T0195819

DON'T GIVE UP!

Lawrence Lloyd Bruckner, ESQ.

authorHOUSE®

AuthorHouse™
1663 Liberty Drive
Bloomington, IN 47403
www.authorhouse.com
Phone: 833-262-8899

Published by AuthorHouse 03/31/2021

ISBN: 978-1-6655-1932-8 (sc)
ISBN: 978-1-6655-1930-4 (hc)
ISBN: 978-1-6655-1931-1 (e)

Library of Congress Control Number: 2021904717

Print information available on the last page.

All scriptures were taken from the King James Version. Public Domain.

CREDITS

The following people mentored me on my path:

A. 1961-1969, Bernie Voss helped me become the National 4-H Citizenship winner. That scholarship helped pay for the World Campus Afloat world cruise with Chapman College in 1970.

B. 1963-67, John Brigham, science teacher supervised my science projects allowing me to be elected the Vice President of the State Junior Academy of Science. This allowed me to attend the West Virginia Science Camp where I met Senator Randolph of West Virginia who counseled "if you want make a real change in the world, go into politics where you control billions of dollars in research and development".

C. 1964-present: William Gengenbach who helped me to achieve the number 1 agricultural student in Illinois in 1967.

D. 1969: Professor Davis, Trinity College entered me in a private tutorial on leadership and charismatic development.

E. 1970: Professor Campo on Trinity's first Rome campus introduced me the world's classical thought, culture and conquest.

F. Professor Gassman shepherded my MA thesis on governmental rural policies that unintentionally destroyed the American family farm system.

G. 1972: John Williams appointed me as a summer intern to the House Republican Policy Committee where I learned the corrupt influences of money.

H. 1973: George Nichols served as my mentor in developing my law practice in Dixon, IL.

I. 1981: Married my wife, Luanne, my secret high school sweetheart and companion.

J. 2020 Nancy Bruckner Spinelli, BA Trinity 1974, who typed this book. K. 1990 Brianna Bruckner, Eureka 2012 BA, St. Thomas, 2018 MIB, my daughter, my love and motivation for writing this book.

Lloyd and Mildred Bruckner, my parents, celebrated their 40th wedding anniversary before Lloyd was taken ill. They are nothing, but united with millions of Americans, they represent the "miracle dream generation".

Lloyd, a native of Wisconsin and blind in one eye and with only an eighth-grade education, volunteered in 1942 as an Army Air Corps machinist. In 1941 he had attended trade school from 11 p.m. until 7 a.m. six days per week, to learn his trade. He built machines (airplanes) to save America and after the war, machinist built the machines that produced our cars, tractors, etc., the real wealth of America.

Mildred, graduated from high school and worked for a hospital in Hillsboro, WI. However, seeing the hospitals clogged with wounded soldiers, she entered nursing training at Mayo's School of Nursing where she received her R.N. She worked six hours a day as an aide and attended school 4 hours a day, six days a week. After receiving her degree, she went to Sacramento, CA to work in the hospital there. In 1946, Wisconsin natives met in Sacramento, subsequently married and moved to Savanna, IL where they raised three children.

Starting with a 22-acre plot of sand, they expanded to a 400-acre dairy farm. Both labored intensely on their little plot of ground and milked 70 cows on their farm while Lloyd worked a fulltime job. They raised watermelons as a side crop.

They achieved all of their goals without government assistance. All they wanted in life was to live in peace and to build a better place of their children. They never gave up even in the most trying of times.

DEDICATION

This book is dedicated to my Mother and Father
who worked and sacrificed so that their children
could have better lives than they did.

INTRODUCTION
Why I wrote this book?

It is October of 2020. In my three scores plus 10 years of life and forty years as a stepfather, I am writing this collection of thoughts focusing on information that I wish someone had passed on to me. Life is a river. Use this handbook for insight and reflection. The information may save you from drowning or at least smooth the rough waters. I always think of the quotes: "Those who ignore history are condemned to repeat it." and "Insanity is doing the same thing over and over again and expecting different results."

Hopefully you are sane, will have the WILL to try different approaches to life's challenge: Stop often, do the exercises, relate to your personal position on the River and TAKE time to observe and help others. Relationships provide the paradigm for reference. Without relationships with people, you run the risk of going in circles and not realizing you are. One day you wake up realizing you have wasted time, i.e. your life. Stay focused and enjoy the ride. There is no turning back the clock. You only get one ride down the River of Life.

This book is written in three parts:

Part I. Recipe for Living

This one is targeted for the 12-30 year old readers. It basically gives fatherly advice to my daughter, who graduated from Eureka College in 2012. (It is where President Reagan graduated with a degree in Sociology in 1932.)

Part II: The Book

This part is designed to reflect on the Bible (Greek word for The Book). It follows a pathway of explaining a course of action for 30-60 year-old people who used the knowledge from Part I to build a home filled with love, peace, harmony, growth and redemption.

Part III: Path Away from Hell

After living 60 years growing and working, this part is defensive. It builds on Parts I and II with policies, programs and actions that will protect and steer away from Hell here on earth. With planning, conservation and applied wisdom resulting from the wisdom section engrained in Part I, the wise will reduce the isolation, depression and pain endured during the winter of our existence.

Memorize these pillars of life:

I. DEATH IS CERTAIN

Everything is born, grows, matures and dies. The good die. The bad die also. Hopefully, you developed option A, B,

C from the first book so your family can survive. PLAN your funeral and do your estate planning NOW!!!

II. YOU ONLY HAVE THIS MOMENT, TIME IS MORE IMPORTANT THAN WEALTH

We cannot go back. Do good NOW to have pleasant memories. We can go forward but by taking full advantage of NOW, your dreams of tomorrow can become the joy of today.

III. YOU ONLY CONTROL 100% OF ONE PERSON.

If it is to be, it is up to me. You can influence, restrict, help others but you only control yourself 100%. Unless others want to change you, you are wasting your time trying to control them. Set a good example.

IV. PRACTICE, DO PROJECT WITH LOVE AND MERCY

By giving 10% of your time as unattached action, you nurture the seed for love and understanding for people you never knew. Practice mercy. DO NOT spend time or energy trying to win or get revenue. Forgive those who trespass upon you but remember WHY it happened.

V. LET THE FORCE BE WITH YOU

We are animals. Speech and abstract thought are a wonderful projection of the holy spirit, the FORCE, ghost, psychic projection or whatever name we want to describe it by. While the forgoing brings purpose to our "organized" environment, the animal spirits are still there. Practice and practice to stream the senses of sight, smell, taste, feeling, the urge to reproduce, etc. Follow your instincts. The conscious mind will not understand but a focused, trained unconscious force will strengthen your soul.

HOW HAS THE WORLD CHANGED SINCE 1900

- Ninety percent of all US physicians had no college education; instead, they attended medical schools, many of which were condemned in the press and by the government as "substandard".
- Sugar cost four cents a pound; coffee 15 cents a pound and eggs were 14 cents a dozen.
- The population of Las Vegas, Nevada was 30 people.
- Crossword puzzles, canned beer and iced tea hadn't been invented.
- Only 6% of all Americans had graduated from high school; one in ten US adults couldn't read or write.
- Eighteen percent of households in the US had at least one full-time servant or domestic.
- Marijuana, heroin and morphine were all available over the counter at corner drugstores. "Heroin clears the complexion, gives buoyancy to the mind, regulates the stomach and the bowels, and is, in fact, a perfect guardian of health."

This is past, now start the journey down the River of Life!!!

CONTENTS

PART I

Turning Points of History 2

Cycles of Living Are Like A Spiral 10

Don't Worry, Be Happy 13

Live Your Life to the Fullest Now! 15

Motivators 21

Health 26

Water 29

Stress 35

Wisdom 37

Knowledge 41

What You Must Retain from Your Eureka Education 43

Occupation 57

Entrepreneur 62

Investing 71

Taxes 75

Saving Tips 78

Skills 84

Summary 89

Conclusion 96

PART II

Genesis 98

Exodus 100

Leviticus, Numbers, Deuteronomy 104

Joshua 107

Judges, Ruth, Samuel I, II; Kings I, II, Chronicles 111

Ezra, Nehemiah, Esther, Job 114

Proverbs 119

Ecclesiastes 124

Jeremiah, Lamentations, Isaiah 128

Ezekiel 26, Daniel 28 130

Obadiah, Jonah, Micah, Nabium, Habakkuk,
Zephaniah, Haggai, Zechariah, Malachi 137

The Gospels 139

Acts 140

Corinthians I and II, Galatians 145

Ephesians 148

Philippians and Colossians 150

Thessalonians I and II 153

Timothy, Titus and Philemon 155

Hebrews & James 159

Peter I, Ii 161

Epistle of John And Jude 163

Revelations 167

PART III

Introduction to Part III 172

Why People Fear Retirement 174

Roadmap 177

Remember to Keep Needs Small: Planning A $900
Funeral 180

2020 Specific Suggestions for Seniors 182

Health is Our Number One Priority 186

Health Habits: You Are What You Eat 191

Essential Immunity 193

Senior Immune Boosters 195

Pain 196

Apple Cider Vinegar 197

Sleep 198

Relaxed Mind Healthy Body 201

Aging & Energy 202

Where Are We Now??? 206

Investing in an Age of Uncertainty 209

A Penny Saved is a Penny Earned Without Taxes 212

How to Draw a New Path Away from Hell 229

Omega 232

Words of Wisdom 233

Conclusion for Part III 234

INTRODUCTION

The first Part was designed to be a foundation for a young adult. Its emphasis was on building for the future. In following the book of the Bible trying to inspire young people to study the scripture and reflect on how their lives serve a purpose. Without health, there is nothing. This third and final part is for seniors expands the theme in the others and broadens the horizon to use what was presented in the first two parts.

PART I

Recipe for Living

Call L. Bruckner for coaching and questions, 815-259-3168
or bruck175@hotmail.com

TURNING POINTS OF HISTORY

410-800 AD: Decline in West caused by climate, hunger, (people who are hungry have poor immune system, poor sanitation in cities), leads to epidemic in urban areas. People flee to farm destroying commerce – reduces standard of living and reduces productivity because everyone is diverted to provide necessary food, clothing and shelter. Vandals, Germans and Huns from Russian Steppes move south because of cold, hunger; Normans move from Norway to France and Ireland.

Invading tribes had no written language therefore all laws, religion, medicine skills, beliefs were entirely personal. Tribe selected leader who by strength ruled. Since they placed no value on writing and urban society, they found it easier to use or destroy rather than build. Scrolls made excellent starter for fires. Because of their value systems and lack of written schooling, people after 1000 referred to the period after the Vandals invaded Rome in 410 A.D. as the Dark Ages.

632 AD: Mohammed dies, founder of the new Islam – Arabs begin conquest in all directions – trade policy and Islam religion practiced produces excess population that in turn provided soldiers for armies of conquest.

800: Pope crowns Charlemagne Emperor of the Holy Roman Empire. Establishes church supremacy, has vision of renewing the old empire. (Expanded population, growth of schools, interest in preserving information by writing, information and observations written down in books.)

1066 Battle of Hastings – Normans conquer British Isle. – reopen the Island to European influences (Roman IX and X legions in York and Bath left in 410 AD)

1095: Pope Urban II calls for first Crusade – except for brief periods, it never succeeded; unintended consequences stimulated trade and ideas e.g. brought meatballs from Istanbul to Stockholm where they become known as Swedish meatballs.

1206: Genghis Khan becomes hungry and begins the conquest of Asia; he uses strict merit to determine advancement in the army. Stirrups and improved bows give horsemen advantages.

1204: 4th Crusade Western mercenaries capture and sack Constantinople – weakens Greek culture in Asia Minor.

1299: Marco Polo returns to Venice having served Kublai Khan (and brought pasta to Italy) – this expands trade and ideas allowing Genoa (Columbus' birthplace) and Venice to develop as commercial centers.

1453: Constantinople is captured by Turks – Europe looks west and south by water to find new way to India and China since trade routes are all controlled by Muslims. Now we have the new Belt and Road initiative of the Chinese Liberation Army to reestablish the trade connections of China to the West.

1492: Columbus lands in what he always considered "India", later Amerigo Vespucci working for the Medici Family (wealthy Florentine bankers), produces a map which he claims was NOT India but a New Continent which he named for himself: America!

1512: Portuguese finally reach Moluccas, a Spice Island in modern Indonesia. Water transportation is much cheaper than land. It is cheaper to move a bushel of wheat from Spain to Syria than to load it on a cart and move 50 miles inland to Sparta, Greece.

1518: Smallpox introduced in Hispaniola – European diseases kills natives; western germs conquer Americas –allowing Europeans to settle and expand west

1519: Cortez returns as God Quetzalcoatl, conquers Mexico – gold flows to Europe just in time to finance western mercenaries and stop Turkish conquest of Europe in Austria and Bohemia.

1522: 18 out of 250 men return to Spain from Magellan's world trip – proves the world is round.

1543: Copernicus's paper published after death calculating rotation of our sun and spinning on axis – put Sun at center not the Earth.

1580: Spanish Armada defeated by storm and England; England rises, Spain declines.
Allows North America to be English and French.

1602: Dutch East Indies Co – 18% annual dividend for almost 300 years produced primarily by spice trade.

1500-1600: Numerous attempts to find Northwest Passage to India (all failed) route to China after fall of Greek Empire in 1452.

1600: Movable type makes books cheaper and abundant. Luther reformation succeeds because there were the tools to print the Bible. Increased population causes expanded demand. Wealth (codfish for protein) and products (potatoes and corn) from America allow quality of living to improve.

1700: Industrial Revolution takes hold – Steam Power allows increased productivity, greater demand for coal that is needed because the expanded population in England had used all the forest reserves for fuel. People need coal to stay warm – expanded labor force; raised value of labor increased because of productivitiy. Shifted wealth based on land holdings to wealth earned from industry and trade. Specialization of labor increases productivity—many inventions, discoveries, experiments becomes known as the industrial revolution..

1762: First clock at sea to work without effects of temperature, rotation, gravity.
Navigation improvement allows better ships, more travel, and safer journeys.
Profits for traders; expands wealth and ideas.

1776: Thirteen out of twenty British colonies declare independence from King George III – based on written rule of law, self government, enlightenment, scientific inductive reasoning, separation of church and state (government). Developed three separate co-equal branches of government-Executive, Congress, and Judiciary.

1777: Battle of Saratoga, Benedict Arnold saves the Colonies – British are defeated -- convinced French to aid Colonies – Dutch financing. The American experiment begins after French fleet block British retreat at Yorktown, VA.

1789: US Constitution adopted (French Revolution: weakened nobility & Church's power). British have coal from their mines and food from N.A. (especially cod from the Great Bank offshore on Nova Scotia, Canada). French has population growth and no new protein sources – Let them eat cake doesn't work when there is no wheat.

1803: Louisiana Purchase – Napoleon gives up on New World. US doubles in size; later Monroe Doctrine establishes America for Americans.

1805-1815: Trafalgar, Borodino, Waterloo: destroy Napoleon (British & Russia won).
Art of War changes from mercenaries and professional soldiers to draftees and citizen's armies; War of 1812 ends as Britain finally realizes U.S.A. is lost with the Treaty of Ghent. Europe if fragmented and reunification does not start until Bismarck and the Prussians develop the modern state of Germany in 1870.

1807: Fulton steam engine works (new mode of transportation) water and rail

1825: First practical railroad begins in London, England.

1831-1836: Darwin collects samples; later develops theory of natural selection – new paradigm for biology.

1837: British patent for electric telegraph – Morse develops code and motor – greatly expands speed of sending information.

1854: Perry opens Japan's ports (trade expands in ALL of EAST) – European power forces trade in China along rivers.

1864: War Between the States July 4, 1863 – South lost war at Gettysburg because of poor communications; their support of slavery stops any foreign recognition or intervention. Northern wheat is more important than Southern cotton.

1903: First airplane at Kitty Hawk, NC by Wright Brothers: faster transportation;

Ford works on assembly line to mass produce cars: to use unskilled labor to do one task faster and better than skilled craftsmen.

1904: Russia loses war to Japan – peace brokered by Theodore Roosevelt shook the West and inspires the East to embrace Japan which leads to WW II. "Asia for the Asian": The West gradually transfers control of trade and technology to the East. The Eastern powers have no concept of patents or protections of intellectual property in contract to the west; stealing is not punished but rewarded in the Oriental society.

1909-11: North Pole reached by Peary; Norwegian Amundsen reaches South Pole: man has reached all land points; now starts exploration of ocean floor.

1914: Panama Canal opens. Along with Suez Canal (in the 1870's), it expands trade. WW I begins August 1.

1918: War changes everything; all events after November 11, 1918 at 11 A.M. are causally connected to the unintentional consequences of the WAR to END ALL WARS; i.e. Communist takeover in Russia sweeps away Monarchy and Sultans; submarines and airplanes change sea warfare. Tanks, poison gas, trucks and communication change land warfare. The Austrian-Hungarian Empire and the Ottoman Empire are forced to dissolve into either independent states or territories controlled by the French and British.

1939: September 1: Germany invades Poland which starts WW II; Hitler's National Socialism awakens the "VOLK" in German culture that continues to grow today.

1941-1945: December 7: Japanese bomb Pearl Harbor, Russia stops the German advance in Stalingrad (1942), the U.S. stops Japan's Navy at Midway and Coral Sea, the Allied Forces invade Normandy in France (1944); the Marines take Iwo Jima in preparation to invade Japan. Atomic bomb is used; the new power source changes the balance of power. $E=Mc^2$.

1944: Brentwood Treaty sets the world currency exchange until Nixon takes the US off of the gold standard in 1971. US dollar replaces the British pound as reserve currency.

1945: UN founded – placed in NY – goal is to stop ALL aggressive wars. (Works until US violates the treaty and invades Iraq in 2003.) Jewish people get homeland, sanctioned in 1948 – Start new crusade.

1949: Chairman Mao Zedong – controls mainland China which revolutionizes Chinese culture, ends elite's status and Mongol power is replaced by People's Republic Army (Chinese).

1950: World population 2.5 billion (now 6.5 billion); Cannot sustain growth to 2050 (estimated at 9.0 billion) without cheaper energy, more cultivated land and increased productivity from oceans.

1954: French lost Dien Bien Phu in Vietnam and like Japanese victory over Russia in 1904 shows that the West can be defeated. This is the beginning of the end for Western dominance in Asia.

1957: Sputnik I: first space satellite – new frontier.

1961: First man in space: Russian – shows man can live in space.

1966: Venera III: a Russian probe is the first human object to land on another planet.

1969: July 20: Neil Armstrong (USA) is first man on the moon: "This is one small step for a man, one giant leap for mankind."

1973: US loses Vietnam War (psychological defeat). The message to West: move out of Asia.

1974: Arab uses oil as economic weapon – results in massive inflation to stimulate Western economy and starts massive borrowing and printing of paper currencies by government to transfer wealth from the savers to the poor via inflation.

1982:   American recession forces Reagan to "borrow" massive amounts of money to continue US bubble, accelerates manufacturing shift to cheaper labor markets overseas. This allows Chinese labor to compete with Japanese production.

1989:   Berlin Wall torn down – ends Cold War. Capitalism provides greater productivity and flexibility; opens vast new markets in suppressed Eastern Europe and creates short term economic expansion especially for Germans. Encourages expanded credit bubble that in turn creates unsustainable debts.

CYCLES OF LIVING ARE LIKE A SPIRAL

You need to study the various cycles of living that are outlined in Part III. Especially study Marstrose who promotes an 8.6 year economic conference model. I will make it very simple for you. In 2021 we are in the late stages of many cycles. Unless we continue to have major technological breakthroughs the expanded stress of over population will make it harder to maintain the current standard of living. The elite will continue to expand their control of the current systems until one of the ancient four horsemen (hunger, drought, disease, and war) collapses civilization as we know it.

Now you have the historical benchmarks. How does that

affect living today? It does because life reflects the balances of many forces. Some we realize, others are too big, complex or distant for a human to appreciate, let alone understand. For example, one of the defining moments in my life was looking through a telescope at Trinity College in Hartford, CT at what I thought was a star in the sky. Looking through the scope, I discovered it was NOT a star but a distant galaxy consisting of millions of stars.

We now know our Sun is an average star rotating with other suns that rotate around the center of one galaxy that rotates with other galaxies. While you only control yourself, your existence and your navigation down the river of life, there are determining forces that follow patterns (cycles) that affect the amount of water in the river, therefore affecting its temperature, speed, clarity, and salinity which in turn affects its ability to sustain life. As you live, you need to do three things:

A. Study the past to see how people responded to cycles
B. Study the past to determine cycles that predict trends: 500 years, 54 years, 4 years, 1 year
C. Record personal defining moments in your life and write down how and why that experience (adventure) affected your being and changed your course on the River of Life.

Concerning point A: compare an average American in 1901 to one today: in 1901, the life expectancy was 47 now it's 78.4. Only 8% of households had a telephone, now nearly everyone has one. Internet now is accessed by over 60% of the population today. There was no radio, TV or computer, now nearly everyone has one. There were only 8000 cars. The average worker earned 10 cents per hour; now Illinois' minimum wage is rising to $15 by 2023 causing wage inflation. California had 1.4 million people (less than Iowa); now more than 30 million.

What are the trends? These include increased population, denser population in cities, and intense demand for resources. Now put that on a world scale where today the US at 6% of the world population consumes 35-40% of the world resources. What happens when the rest of the world wants the same standard of living as the US??? Will technology save us or will the demand pressure push humanity back to the old standard of stealing from one another to survive.

B. What trends can be ascertained? We are at the end of a 500 year cycle. Over the next 100 years, there will be a shift from West to East. Baby boomers (those born between 1946-1964) are past their production phase. They will be consuming wealth especially health care goods and services. (3) Fossil fuels are still the cheapest energy source but environmental costs are now starting to be realized. Without a tech breakthrough, energy consumption will rise as well as the cost. (4) Federal government has inflated the currency and expanded credit, (housing, credit cards, government loans both domestic and foreign). One trillion more in student loans--wow. The problem is masked by the government refinancing debt by pushing the repayment off until later. Today the government borrows (or prints currency) for 40 cents on every one dollar spent! Can governments again expand credit that determines prices? Once that trend ends, you may have to change direction.

C. Remember for history to be relevant, you NEED to personalize history. Write down defining moments and HOW and WHY they affected <u>YOU</u>.

DON'T WORRY, BE HAPPY

Your lifestyle will put all the pieces together. You must understand happiness. Although man's main motivation is to avoid PAIN (not to be eaten), it is the pursuit of happiness that brings fulfillment and purpose to living.

Happy people like themselves. Look at your total existence and determine how you are going to act. Studies conclude external circumstances have little effect on psychological well-being. Four inner traits foster a happy lifestyle: socializing, sense of personal control, optimism, and self esteem.

Socializing is easy for extroverts who "appear" to be happier. The <u>key</u> is to give 10% of you to something NOT BENEFITING YOU. The act of giving releases you into the environment around you and forces you to interact. Maybe it is caring for a dog, reaching out or helping clean the public park, doing something with the church or social organization such as the Lions Club (Liberty, Intelligence, Our Nation's

Safey), going to talk to a neighbor, your family, or people in a nursing home: give 10% to something.

Personal control leads to satisfaction. People in prison, nursing homes, factories, or colleges suffer lower morale, greater stress and worse health because they lack a sense of personal control. Gain control by first stop worrying: 90% of the things you worry about you cannot affect anyway, so forget it. Focus on effective time management. Write down a daily schedule of your challenges and how you are going to deal with them. Do leave time for personal FUN activities YOU enjoy. Reward yourself for little successes on a daily basis.

Smile and be optimistic. Hope is definitely not the same as optimism. It is not conviction that something will turn out correctly but knowing something makes sense and is good regardless of the ending. In reality, there is 4 oz of water in a 12 oz glass. To be happy, say to yourself, the glass is one third full and I'm thinking about how to make it two thirds full. Don't Worry, Be Happy.

Fourth and finally, like yourself. By following the Golden Rule "Do unto others as you would have them do onto you", this should give you a framework or paradigm on how others respond to you. By knowing yourself, you should be able to figure out what you like and what you dislike. Strengthen your likeness and CHANGE what you dislike regardless of peer pressure, family, etc. Look in the mirror—who do you see—the only person who can make it happen: YOU!!!

LIVE YOUR LIFE TO THE FULLEST NOW!

Tapping side of head below the nose, chin below the couth and center of chest resets the nerves.

Set a regular time to wake up each day. If you have a partner, spend a few minutes enjoying each others companionship. Get up; massage your body all over. Stretch the muscles and joints: do exercises (in the following section are examples of exercises). Breathe deeply; expel all the air you can. If possible, have ferns and other plants in your living area. They filter air and produce oxygen.

Have bright colors in your dwelling. Have some plants to care for and something that depends on you for support, i.e. children, neighbors, pets, etc.

After dressing, drink a glass of "good" water and have a peaceful breakfast to stimulate the digestive tract. Read the section on nutrition.

Follow the exercises with getting ready for the day. Avoid washing your skin too often as the floride and water washes away vital oils that protect your skin; remember that it is the largest organ in your body.

Use sea salt or other natural products to brush teeth. It is more important to floss and remove particles between your teeth. Floss before bed and after eating breakfast. Scrape your tongue to remove harmful microbes entering your gut.

I repeat-Have a good breakfast. Stay colorful, eat fruits, juices, oatmeal, nuts, and natural fiber cereals. Reduce carbohydrate intake and caffeine. (NO STARBUCKS.) Increase your PURE WATER intake. Have one glass before eating and another before starting to work. I assume you are producing enough acid to properly digest food. If not, do NOT drink water before meals. Wait and consume water between meals. Try to walk to work. Use stairs instead of elevators, park three blocks away and walk to your destination. Increasing physical activities is the goal. You do not need expensive workout gyms or equipment. *JUST DO IT!* If possible, do it with a spouse or a friend to add enjoyment.

Develop a routine at work or school that reduces stress. Make sure the environment is healthy: good lighting, extra ventilation, clean air, and reduced noise. If possible, have music and plants. Baroque music improves memory. Mozart is my favorite.

During the day, refocus your soul by using a simple sequence developed centuries ago. Massage the end of the nerve meridian at the inside of your eyebrow first above the nose on the right side of the head. After 30 seconds, then massage the point at the base bordering the outside of your left eye. Then go to the bone under the eye about 1" below your pupil. Proceed to the area between the bottom of your nose and your mouth. Following that massage, do the same to the point about half -way between your lower lip and the bottom of your chin. During the day, repeat the process if under stress. The same procedure can be followed on the chest starting opposite the heart above the nipple. Massaging along the nerve meridian helps to stimulate nerve energy level and reset body functions. The procedure can also be used in prayer or meditation sessions to help stabilize body functions.

Use your break to get SUNLIGHT, outside air, bathroom and water. Avoid too much caffeine—NO ARTIFICAL SWEETENERS. If they allow smoking breaks, do not smoke but go outside with them to walk and stretch joints. Stimulate your gray cells with puzzles, reading and visualize your next dream.

Eat SMALL PORTIONS. DO NOT skip lunch. Eat colorful antioxidants (fruits and vegetables), eat natural. Stay away from <u>white</u> bread, pastas and sugars.

These are food that help reduce illness. For your liver eat grapefruits, avocados, bananas, garlic, cabbage.. To reduce diabetes consume berberine, magnesium, green tea, mulberry leaf, AMPK, chromium, cinnaman, biotin, PGX, ALA, pegnogenol, Vitamin D3, selenium, Vitamin K, and probiotic to protect the gut. In my opinion to guard against breast cancer use thyme oil, cinnaman, jasmine and chaminole. For protection against the numerous cancers, in my opinion, use glutathione NAC, alpha lipids, zinc and seleinium. Take crill oil and arthonium to protect your eyes. Check your iodine level to boost your thyroid gland function.

To help you remember what to eat, remember G(bombs) equals greens, beans, onions, mushrooms, beets, seeds (walnuts and Brazililan nuts).

Avoid isolation at work and home. We are animals. We function best in a "pack" tribal environment. Remember to give the 10% talked about earlier. Try to network with fellow workers either thru the union, group projects, camping, ball team etc. If it does not exist, take an activity you enjoy and try to get others to "buy in". Getting people to visit your church is a way to positively expand your networking capacity.

Regardless of the type of work or schooling you do, you and you alone control the mental monologue going on in your head. To get fancy, we call it cognitive restructuring. To tame toxic thoughts, breathe deeply and HOLD IT. Take three breaths and then go forward. Ask yourself key questions like what can I really do about this? In answering your questions, use past experiences. Reframe the situation as <u>a series of small problems with a positive answer</u>. If still negative, STOP the process and go to another TOPIC in your mind.

If you do not like the scientific approach above, simply recite the 23rd psalm (which is very soothing) and write down the problems or task. Tell yourself what you are going to do about reducing PAIN and increasing happiness for your boss and co-workers.

If you spend a lot of time on the road, use the radio and recordings to relax, learn and expand your horizons. When you get home from work (whether it is a job, school, or housework at home), take time to change clothes, and exercise. <u>Play</u> with other household members (interaction is key: eating together, group games, sports, exercise, etc.)

Take time to relax, write down the next day's schedule, plan ahead and work six days and save one day either for God or Yourself. Rest one day and do different things from the other six days.

Think about something positive. I avoid the news and weather because it tends to be "crisis oriented". (No need to stress about something a thousand miles away that you cannot control.

Look at life as a glass half full rather than half empty. Have a "Humor Eye": keep funny cartoons, pictures, memories of situations that *MAKE YOU HAPPY*. Handle the unpleasant with an escape humor mantra. For example, I have a line for crises: my schedule is full and I refuse to be intimidated by realty. I personally use a simple one from Star Trek when I am frustrated: Beam me up, Scotty.

The above simple daily routine emphasizes the major points expressed throughout the book. What all the effort is designed to accomplish is to modulate the "FLOW" down the River of Life.

You want to achieve a state of consciousness where your involvement and concentration makes the "job" worth it for its own sake. You achieve a state where you are being carried away by the force that makes what you are doing seem effortless and automatic.

The "Flow" state is NOT achieved to accomplish another goal. It is a state of being at peace. It is the one thing I miss most about retiring from my law practice. Counseling my people, and visualizing their pain, feelings, and hopes made the time fly. I would start at 1 PM and be shocked it was 5 PM and time to go home. Flow is different for everyone. Some people must use rituals to put their mind on automatic pilot and ease them into a state of concentration. Some athletes have a warm up schedule that gets them going. Some surgeons have the same breakfast routine for preparing for the operation that sets the mode. Whatever it takes, the ride is wonderful. People, who tell me they cannot do it, won't do it. It requires getting over a sense of self consciousness. If you are self centered, you are prevented from concentrating on anything except yourself. The key is to find the right task and you will never "work" again.

In closing, I copied this story that crystallizes better than I on how to live.

A Parable to Live By

I still remember opening my aunt's "hope chest". She never married. I lifted out a tissue wrapped package. Inside was an exquisite hand-made scarf trimmed with handcrafted, cobweb lace. It had been gifted for her marriage by her grandmother. She never wore it, saving it for a "special" occasion that never came. Her death was the only occasion left to wear it.

My wife took the scarf from me with the other clothes that we were taking to the mortician. The silk was soft and smooth as I quickly slammed the lid closed. DON'T EVER SAVE ANYTHING FOR A SPECIAL OCCASION!!!!!! Remember every day is a special occasion. I was deeply depressed thinking of all the things she had not seen, heard or done. I pondered over things she had done, not realizing that they were special. I had a *Eureka!* moment as I now spend more time with the family. Cleaning, dusting or worrying about appearances are not as important. Life should be a pattern of experiences to save, not to endure. Don't save anything. Use the fine articles now.

Forget the habit of putting off tasks, do it now! The more I think, the more I realize putting off calling friends, writing letters, telling my wife and children the value to me should be done TODAY, not someday. Time is limited. Remember the five rules of life in the introduction. I thank my precious

Aunt Mary for opening my eyes. I am trying hard not to procrastinate. Plan for tomorrow but live for today as if it is your last day on Earth. Smile, add laughter and luster to the spice of life! Every moment, every breadth is a gift from God.

MOTIVATORS

In the last part, we discussed lifestyle. Good habits engraved early make it easier to establish a stable, healthy lifestyle that is sustainable. The Roman Catholic knows this; so many resources are used in their schools to engrain habits.

Before exploring the priorities of living, you need to ponder where you are in the cycle of life. These basic life motivations explain why your peers are motivated to do what they do. They will determine what motivates YOU in the 80 year cycle of life.

```
              / \
           /Exist 80\
           /Health 70\
          / Closure 60\
          / Control 50 \
          / Money 40 \
          / Family 30 \
         / Adventure 20 \
```

STOP and study the pyramid. The steps establish the primary motivations for each decade of living. The pyramid shape shows that your flexibility and capacity for mental and physical extension <u>decreases</u> with age depending on genetics, environment, how much you abuse your body and mind, stress and work demands.

Secondly, the pyramid only shows primary motivators. A 50 year old may still want adventure and freshness while still desiring to control his destiny. The diagram also assumes normalcy. Mental deviates, drug abuse (mind altering drugs) will change normal motivational behavior. If you are different, do not be alarmed; just be aware of the norm. You need to adjust your lifestyle to cope with general patterns. For example, homosexuality is not the norm. It is not necessarily bad for you, but it is considered bad by a large percentage of the population. You may want to move into or out of a neighborhood because of the "character" of the majority of people living there. Simply use common sense when analyzing a person's subconscious and conscious motivators.

In your 20s, you are young, educated and physically grown. People want to experience new cultures, activities, and lifestyles. Many times they revolt against the ways of their parents and the controls of society.

By 30's, people will "settle down". If they have not married or divorced and remarried, they are desirous of a nest, children and stability both at work and home. Learning from their "adventures" makes the 30 year old wiser, more willing to listen to his elders and more sensitive to his surroundings and other people. Maybe global warming will convince you NOT to have children.

By 40's, the growing demands of a family and the feeling of mortality (retirement) pushes people to try to earn more money, work overtime, etc. Some take a second job, change careers, etc. See section II of the book to discover ways to deal with aging.

By 50's, if they have children, they are teenagers or older, parents are dead or dependent. People feel a loss of control; therefore they strive to control their surroundings and job.

By 60's, the battle is either won or lost. Control and needing more money seem less important. It is a time to start closing down. Retirement forces stress adjustments. Reduced income forces liquidation. Grandchildren cause a person to reflect on what are the <u>real</u> important values and things in life. See Section III to cope with the winter of your existence.

By 70's, health overtakes all other concerns. Friends and siblings are dying. People have less energy. The senses, especially taste, sight and hearing are noticeable <u>reduced</u>.

If you make it to 80 and beyond, your wisdom, habits and lifestyle have satisfied your wants and needs. Your happiness has taught you to hope. You have accepted your place in the universe. You do not need this book. You should be writing your own book for your grandchildren's benefit before you get dementia or expire.

Finally, do not forget some people never "grow up". For a series of reasons, we do not have room to discuss why some people become fixated at a certain level or change at different ages. Some men at 60's are 20 year old adventurers and never change.

SECRET: *Do not try to change people's motivators. You CAN NOT change them; only the person can change themselves. Believe me, I have tried and FAILED.*

From a health standpoint if you are still in school, keep your mind on your studies, athletics, arts and science. Use your time to develop NEW skills, life habits, and READ, READ, READ. If you have extra energy, get a job, and save money for college. If college is NOT for you, then SAVE TO BUY A HOUSE. Keep your mind off of sex and try to avoid TV and movies that sell sex, sex, and more sex. Do not rush life; you will be old soon enough. Save a few joys for later; you will be happier.

If you are an adult, you have to understand these facts: 70% of men think about sex every day while only 35% of women think about sex every day. Only 28% of women want more sex in their lives and 40% of men want more. The average married couple has sex 58 times a year while couples under 30 have sex 111 times a year. (I told you it was popular.) 59% of women claim they enjoy sex a great deal while 83% of men do. Average heterosexuals have 17 partners in their life while the average homosexual has over 500.

After handling over 800 divorces, my advice is simple. One, be very careful who you date. Avoid physical relationships because of the spread of diseases (AIDs). The more persons you or your partners have been exposed to, the more viruses you can get in your body.

Two, stay faithful in a marriage. The grass always looks greener on the other side. Work place tensions are increasing, putting increased stress on marriages. TV and computers, etc divide the family, undermine authority and expose everyone to "advertisements" that look exciting and FUN. Avoid temptation and keep away from potential sources (hot tubs, convention parties, taverns, etc).

Three, keep your life simple, and stay out of debt. All too often, financial problems lead to conflict and break up a marriage.

Four, when you find the "right partner", take care of him/her. Sex is a part of a relationship. Think of it as a plant that needs fertilizer, water, sunshine, and time to grow. Make your sex experience FUN, try different things, TALK to your partner about the experience. Stay healthy and use sex as an extension of your exercise plans.

Fifth, set a "date night" even if you have been married 40 years.

Six, relax and be happy. Don't believe the braggart about their "accomplishments". Seven, touch and massage yourself and your partner. Mentally visualize where you want to be, with time, and practice, you will get there if not physically, at least spiritually. In closing, I want you to remember the reason for sex is to produce children. Society has encouraged reproduction by sanctifying marriage and it works too well. We suffer from overpopulation. Nonetheless, remember that men have different reasons for marriage than women. Keep this in mind when dating and picking a mate.

Women want companionship, security, children, family, and sex in that order. Men want companionship, sex, family, money, and then children. Notice BOTH SEXES WANT A BUDDY to share their experiences.

SECRET: *when selecting a mate, analyze the friendship, likes, and dislikes, social, economic, educational and class status. Check out relatives, parents, etc; if they are NOT compatible, then sex, children and money will NOT overcome the lack of companionship.* (Remember I did 800 divorces. Biggest complaint: "I hate the jerk.") Also notice money is NOT the same as women's security. Men want "two can live cheaper than one" mode. Women want a man that will be her champion (knight) protecting her and her babies. Money helps but it must be more to have a secure marriage.

HEALTH

Those who do not have time for exercise will someday find time for illness and pain.

The best preventive medicine is food and water: you are what you eat! Hippocrates over 2300 years ago stated: "Let food be your medicine." Today no drug company making millions is going to endorse, let alone encourage, anyone to stop taking drugs. Studies show that our immune system will probably balance most problems without medicine. The pill is quicker and corrects the symptoms but the cause is probably nutrition or environmental. More people equal more toxins.

Read "STALE FOOD V. FRESH FOOD" by Robert Ford. For buying herbs, contact Herbal Healer at Mountain View, AR at 870-269-4177

/ \

```
         / \
      / Skills \
     ./Knowledge\
     / Wisdom \
     / Health \
```

The diagram above prioritizes the forces that determine the priorities in living. Without health, NOTHING ELSE MATTERS. Let's build a foundation.

We are animals that originated from the sea. Because sea water is fluid, it contains many constantly changing minerals and compounds needed to survive. Being from Illinois, far from the sea, is an example of an area where there are iodine and selenium deficiency. It is better to eat from the oceans which is why so much of the world population lives near the sea. (When we put mercury and other heavy metals in the oceans, then these toxins override the value of the food.) Do you know where your food comes from? And no, the answer is NOT the grocery store!

As an animal before farming, we were gatherers. We ate berries, nuts, roots, eggs, and meat when there was a kill. Starvation was <u>always</u> a concern. Humans lived near a clean mineralized fresh water supply catching fish, frogs, bugs, etc from the rivers. Food was not cooked but eaten fresh or dried. Later we pickled it with salt, vinegar and sugar.

Remember our evolution. We are victims of our success. Over consumption, radiation, genetic modification, processing, coloring, artificially extending shelf life, etc ALL have a price. The point is to stay close to nature, avoid processed food regardless of the millions of dollars spent on telling you how good it tastes, how sweet it is, how it makes life convenient (pop in the microwave!).

Good health requires YOU to reach a mental, physical, social, and spiritual balance that is right for YOU. Following are guidelines. Experiment, use moderation, get sunshine 10 to 15 minutes a day, and know what you are eating. Read the labels. DO NOT TRUST ANYONE WITH YOUR HEALTH.

Before discussing what goes into the body, remember it is important to know how it goes in. First, do breathing exercises everyday. Breathe ten deep breaths, then breathe five full breaths and expel everything you can. Hold: then empty lungs until you feel the burn. After these five, do ten more slow relaxing breaths, strengthening the diaphragm.

Second, relearn to CHEW your food. Use both sides of the mouth. Open wide but close circular muscles of the mouth firmly and chew at least ten times before swallowing.

Thirdly, I cannot release the secret exercises in this treatise. Suffice it to say, YOU MUST exercise all the ring muscles in the body. Proper exercising of the sphincters is linked to the diaphragm and lordosis (inward curvature of spine in lower back and neck.) Add to this the Tibetan's exercises: they spin ten times right, then ten times left after elongating spine and loosening shoulder muscles that support lungs and head. Just because you exercise, you still need two or three long fast walks per week to strengthen heart muscles, flush veins and energize kidneys and intestines.

Your quality of life depends 25% on your DNA and 75% on your lifestyle and environment; the quality of your air, water, food. Many studies boil it down to two simple markers.

One: keep your weight within the guidelines for your height and frame. Two is to eat a whole food plant-based diet, preferably organic food. Avoid sugars, artificial sweeteners, and excessive caffeine and alcohol. It is that simple.

WATER

You should consume 5 to 7 glasses of live, non-chlorinated water a day depending on your exercises, work activity, humidity and temperature. If it's a hot day, drink more! Each person is different, demands are different. Kidney efficiency is variable so there is no hard and fast rule. The point is that most people do not drink enough water; if you wait until you feel thirsty, chances are, you are already slightly dehydrated. Dehydration produces free radicals which reduce amino acids from protein and suppresses the immune system. Water flushes out toxic wastes and helps regulate body temperature.

Drink more water and less soft drinks or caffeinated beverages. Water with a Ph of 9.0 or higher aids in metabolizing stored fat. Water helps digestion, suppresses your appetite and prevents dehydration. Water is calorie-free, inexpensive and readily available. Substitute sparkling water for alcoholic drinks.

Use natural apple cider vinegar. It replaces toxic home cleaners and can be used internally and externally for pains.

Use honey as a replacement for sugar. Like the Egyptians, use it as a natural bacteria killer.

Stay with natural foods. You start with a wholesome breakfast such as whole grains with bananas and nuts or soluble fiber cereals like steel cut or old-fashioned rolled oats (organic so you don't have the glyphosate). Beans, lentils, and legumes are all good. Remember in the beginning, we gathered berries (strawberries, blueberries, raspberries), and picked fruit off trees (apples, pears, peaches). Eat the whole fruit rather than the juice (juice has <u>more calories and less fiber</u>). Eat organic eggs twice per week.

ALWAYS EAT BREAKFAST, make your noon meal the "Big Meal", then have a light supper.

Keep your plate colorful with dark green leafy vegetables, cruciferous vegetables, tomatoes, squash, mangoes, broccoli, mushrooms and beans (all kinds). Use extra virgin olive oil, avocado oil or coconut oil for cooking and on salads. Eat grass-fed beef, free range eggs, organic milk, yogurt and cottage cheese. Don't forget to eat wild fish two times weekly.

Because of chemical farming, we have artificially increased the quantity of food. GMO and scientific modifications of seeds has created an unsustainable production of food. Unfortunately greater yields have often meant that the grains contain less minute minerals and less nutritional value. As the body needs these vital minerals, the brain demands more consumption resulting in added weight.

SECRET: Start every meal with a little healthy fat. I like walnuts and almonds. The fat will slow the digestion of carbohydrates, keep blood sugar stable and more important, and facilitate the absorption of fat-soluble vitamins and nutrients. Keep in mind that they are also high in calories so moderation is the rule.

Two foods, taken in moderation, that are high in anti-oxidants are red wine and <u>dark</u> chocolate (70% cocoa). A glass of wine with dinner (or grape juice but beware the sugar) is good for your heart and a square of chocolate will satisfy your desire for something sweet while still providing health benefits.

Research shows women who consume 1200 mg of calcium from food sources burn fat 20 times faster than those who consume less than 700 mg daily.

I do not want to be sued by McDonald's and Coke, but while fast food chains pretend to introduce healthy foods, the facts are fast foods are: 1) they wreck your blood sugar, 2) they cook with bad fats (polyunsaturated corn oil and trans fats which build up arterial plaque and raise triglycerides, 3) they are loaded with bad fat and salt; McDonald's adds lard to their hamburger to make them juicy and salt masks the inferior taste of poor quality food.

Today, the average American gets 75% of their salt from prepared and processed food and 25% from the saltshaker. Use sea salt at home for minerals from the sea. Stay away from fast food places – pack a lunch to control portions. Add vegetables, nuts and apples with skins.

What about snacks? Here are good substitutes to avoid heart disease and diabetes.

1. Read labels, anything with high fructose corn syrup to sweeten is bad: it actually stimulates your appetite to consume MORE!

2. Substitute the following: for popsicles, eat berries; for ice cream or milkshakes, have a smoothie with plain yogurt and flaxseed; for candy bars, eat peanut butter on whole grain bread in little pieces; for cookies, cakes or pies, eat apple slices with peanut butter, a handful of natural nuts (no salt or sugar); for soda, have sparkling water with fruit juice or lemon for flavoring; for chips, have baked tortilla chips with salsa or air popped popcorn (stay away from microwave popcorn which contains toxic elements).

You are young. Technology over the next ten years will change the world more than it has changed over the last 100 years. Unskilled and semi-skilled jobs will be eliminated. Robots and AI will control the workforce. Even lawyers will be replaced by AI in reviewing contracts. A litigator has a human mote around him/her to protect their job security.

Communication (6G), sensor and chemistry will change everything. We have more scientists alive today than all the scientists living before us. Solid state batteries will make electric vehicles cheaper than gas ones. Graphite and other alloys will be stronger, cheaper and more malleable than steel. Space and the ocean will open whole new mass industries. Cold fusion will provide almost free energy and DNA sequencing will revolutionize medicine.

Before leaving health, it would be amiss to not address why Americans are too FAT. Fat is an essential component of our diet. Fat is necessary for regulating bodily functions, producing hormones, bones and skin. Fat is the <u>natural</u> "appetite regulator". Excess carbohydrate consumption is the real villain in causing obesity. Food fat does NOT make body fat. Eating fat does not raise blood glucose or insulin levels. Carbs increase the glucose in the bloodstream fast. Insulin takes excess glucose out of the blood and converts it to glycogen that is stored in the muscles and liver. The excess is then converted to body fat. Once converted, it is tough to reverse the process and still keep a high energy level. It would be easier if we hibernated like bears, burned stored fat and in the spring, start to fatten up again.

In his book **"Genius Foods: Become Smarter, Happier, and More Productive While Protecting Your Brain for Life,"**

author Max Lugavere recommends the following foods:

- ☐ Extra-virgin olive oil
- ☐ Avocados
- ☐ Blueberries
- ☐ Dark chocolate
- ☐ Eggs
- ☐ Grass-fed beef
- ☐ Dark leafy greens
- ☐ Broccoli
- ☐ Wild salmon
- ☐ Almonds

In summary, stay away from empty calories (white breads and pasta, alcohol, candy and other sweets). Remember color is good, white is bad. White bread and rice have been stripped of nutrients. Go for the real thing such as wild rice, true whole grain breads and pastas. Stay away from saturated (animal products) and trans fats (margarines, commercial baked goods and fast foods). Read the labels. Processed food companies constantly disguise their products to appear good and taste great, using artificial dyes for color and salt, fats and sugar for taste. Beware low fat foods, many times they contain <u>more sugar</u> and corn fructose to make up for the fats that provided the good taste. Reduce the amount of processed foods that you consume. High fructose corn syrup is highly addictive, making it worse than cane sugar. Stevia is a natural sugar that actually contains fiber but has no calories.

Fast carbs are highly-refined grain products. They are "fast" because they contain short chain of molecules that quickly convert to glucose in your bloodstream. Slow carbs contain complicated molecular chains and FIBER. Beware when using the Glycemic Index or GI: you want foods with a LOW GI number but also get the Glycemic LOAD number also. High fiber foods like carrots and potatoes have a high GI number but a LOW GI load. The true impact level on glucose metabolism is the glucose <u>load</u>! A very simple rule of thumb is to eat only 15 g of sugar per day and keep your carbohydrates to six servings (one serving is 1-20 grams, two servings is 20-40, and three servings is 40-60 grams).

Consume more omega-3 oils less omega-6 because the omega-6 is pro-inflammatory. The ratio should be 4:1, for every four units of omega-3 oils eat one unit of omega-6.

When you are under 40 and are healthy, supplements

should not be necessary if you eat the right foods, get exercise and sunshine. In Section II, we will discuss supplements.

Eat mustard family vegetables (cabbage, broccoli, cauliflower, bok choy, brussel sprouts). If you hate vegetables, eat freshly ground flaxseed. Don't forget onions and nuts.

Put 4-6 drops of SSKi- iodine potassium in a glass of water daily. In ALL cases including food (especially wheat products), watch for adverse reactions. If so, STOP intake and try something else. Because of our family history, Brianna will need to check if SSKI causes thyroid suppression. If so, a doctor may need to supplement T4 hormone.

If you plant a garden, consider adding the following herbs: A. Andrographus as a cold medicine B. Cayenne pepper for sore throats; C. garlic for your heart, D. Peppermint to relieve indigestion, E. Rosemary to reduce headaches; F. Sage-to treat cancor sores; G-St.bi John's Wort as a natural antibiotic for infection. H. Thyme-antiseptic mouth wash to kill bacteria; I. Rhodiola-ADAPTOGONE helps normalize body response to stress.

STRESS

Chronic stress simply stated is toxic to your brain. Stress affects multiple parts of the body; it makes it harder to get your necessary restorative sleep; it upsets the balance of the gut bacteria which affects your brain health; it changes the equilibrium in various hormones withing the body and causes inflammation.

Everyone has stress; the perception can be real or imagined. This sets a cascade of events in your body that causes:

- Rapid aging
- Disease
- Muscle loss
- Diabetes
- High blood pressure
- Shrinkage of the memory center (the hippocampus)

Stress can cause inflammation and oxidation; as well as unbalanced neurotransmitters.

Relaxation would reduce these kinds of inflammatory conditions that add to the burden of disease that leads to Alzheimer's disease. Luckily, there are many ways to turn off stress responses. Here are just a few in addition to meditation:

☐ Meditative walking (walking without distractions such as a smart phone)
☐ Deep breathing
☐ Emotional Freedom Technique (Tapping or EFT)
☐ Forest bathing (also called Shinrin-yoku)
☐ Gardening Reflective journaling
☐ Coloring and/or drawing
☐ Listening to music
☐ Grounding or Earthing
☐ Dancing
☐ Meditative eating or tea ceremony

☐ Yoga or stretching
☐ Tai chi, qi gong, or other martial arts

Do something you love to do that makes you feel good; it can be as simple as doing a puzzle, talking with a loved one, playing, dancing or listening to music or even puttering around the house.

The truth is not always the same as the majority decision. — Pope John Paul II

WISDOM

Wissen (vih-sun) is a German verb "to know". You do not get it from reading. Reading and studying provide knowledge. Primary knowledge, you get from observations and experiences. The Germans call this "erfahrung" (air-far-ung). Experience is the basis for wisdom.

Expand your experience, practice observing. Do not simply look, but study and remember the vision. Work on organizing your memory so you can catalog experiences then you can apply the "knowledge" you gain from reading about other people's experiences. Write down your goals and create a roadmap on how to achieve them.

Go out of your comfort zone. Practice utilitarianism (what is the greatest good for the most people). Write down what you really want. Visualize being and doing what you desire. Fantasize by putting yourself into the drama. Make up stories with you as a character and vocalize your participation.

Mature adults make choices and manage their resources to achieve the most important goals.

SECRET: *In applying the above, know what you control. Do not sweat the little things. Keep your needs small. Fake it until you make it. And the 10 most powerful two letter words in the English Vocabulary: IF IT IS TO BE, IT IS UP TO ME!*

You ask HOW do I apply this secret to everyday living. Ask: How do I live and retain the observations and experiences to expand my advancement of wisdom. The best formula is live "large" by the way of the Templar Cross.

A. Take a skill you are good at and practice, practice, practice until you master it, it is automatic, and your flow is controlled. (Some call this the 10,000 hour rule. It takes that much time to be a true Master. The younger you start, the easier it will be. Look, explore, try. Test your natural talents. Observe what your relatives do. Talk to teachers, find a mentor, test your talents against others. Work to find the skill set you can master. For me, it was to be a teacher. As a lawyer, I used my knowledge and taught my clients how the law applied to their problems. My clients loved this approach.

B. Observe. You can learn something from everyone, but seek out the good people you can trust and depend on in battle. Develop a brotherhood based on mutual strength.

As children, we played on the railroad tracks. We had one older girl who always taunted us with her ability to balance herself on one rail and walk down the rail. As hard as we tried, her brother and I could not match her balance. She always won. Finally, it dawned on me if I got on one rail and the brother got on the other rail and we locked hands, we would stabilize each other and walk down the track. It worked! We won and she never wanted to play that game again. Mutual strength can yield results you could not achieve alone.

C. Tell the truth. Sometimes wisdom will require you to disguise or delay the truth for the faithful and the good of society. Use experience to dictate who you trust, then educate them in the skills to improve prosperity and avoid pain.

D. Care for the orphans and children. Do not provide welfare for the lazy and able-bodied. Work with the children for they are the future. This will provide "meaning" to your life.

In living a "wise" life, remember Cicero saying "Saving Thrift is a Great Revenue." Especially in today's society of taxing income, it is better to save a dollar than to earn one. Later, under Skills, read the section on taxes but remember a dollar saved is a dollar earned. A new dollar earned loses 25 to 50% in taxes.

Always have a Plan B and an emergency Plan C. You will

have your vision, your roadmap, and your written goals for one year, five years, life. All that is good, but spend a little time working up a written Plan B. If Plan A fails for any reason, you need to be cross-trained to go to Plan B. I wanted to enter public service but when not elected, I developed a prosperous private law practice as Plan B.

Have an emergency Plan C. Consider your family in constructing a "what if" situation. With your savings, your network and family support, what will I do if I cannot do A or B?

Finally I close with an old anecdote that puts Wisdom into perspective.

"On the street I saw a small girl cold and shivering in a thin dress, with no hope of a decent meal. I became angry and said to God: WHY DID YOU PERMIT THIS?? WHY DON'T YOU DO SOMETHING ABOUT IT? For a while, God said nothing. That night, he replied quietly, I certainly did do something about it. <u>I MADE YOU</u>."

Life is not measured by the number of breaths we take but by the moments that take our breath away. It's what you learn after you know it that counts! Now is a good time to go back to the five rules of life spelled out in the introduction.

KNOWLEDGE

"Nothing in the world can take the place of Persistence. Talent will not. Nothing is more common than unsuccessful men with talent. Genius will not; unrewarded genius is almost a proverb. Education will not; the world is full of educated derelicts. Persistence and determination alone are omnipotent." Calvin Coolidge

The pursuit of knowledge is a lifelong habit. Coolidge summed it up well. Schooling is only an augmentation. The pursuit, the understanding and use of knowledge will improve your judgment and a selection of vehicles to help you down the River of Life. Learning how to ask "Why" and later "Why Not" will give you the onus to guide your soul over the rapids and find the channel so you do not get struck on a sandbar, capsize, or get eaten by predators. To help you "figure things out", here are ports to guide you.

A. Recognize who YOU ARE. Understand your own culture, beliefs, biases, and prejudices. Where you are on the River of Life influences what you see. Unfortunately you cannot see what happened before (that's why history is so important because others before you tell you what they saw on the River). Mathematics and science are so important because those disciplines provide known theorems and landmarks of how the elements are combined, mixed, and tested. Remember bronze is stronger than either brass or tin. Steel is stronger yet more malleable than iron. Understanding your prejudices stops you from being blinded to different opportunities that impedes your progress.

B. Go to the source. Seek out the masters; get as much first hand exposure to the writing of the ones who really did it. Today with TV and computers, societies are molded and controlled by "Big Brother" where facts are filtered, processed and pre-packaged. Get to the source and do your own experiments.

C. Stay hungry. When I was seven, I could NOT get enough books to read. In third grade, the teacher told me to stop giving book reports because I had done 36 (the next member in the class was at 22). Keep the eagerness. DO NOT LET your spouse, job, or social responsibilities divert your hunger.

D. READ. Daily ask yourself what did I learn? How can I use the information to help and grow? Take a course on How to Read, Remember, and Comprehend. Keep a diary or a file of the nuggets of knowledge you have saved. I have a treasure chest of data more valuable to me than gold. Ask: What did I learn today that I did not know.

E. Practice humility. If you have built your self-esteem, mastered your education, and honed your craft so you are a true knight, it is trying to put up with the prejudiced, ignorant, and lazy swine. Nonetheless, practice TWO procedures. You can always learn something from a pig. They have experience, schooling and talent you may want to know. Recognize that what YOU know is only a fraction of what there is to know. Think of the universe as an elephant and you are feeling its tail. NO WAY CAN YOU SEE OR COMPREHEND THE VISION AND CAPABILITIES OF THE WHOLE ANIMAL.

SECRET: You are going to have so much on your plate of life that the boat could easily sink. Learn early to use inductive and deductive reasoning. Like a lawyer, object to everything that is not relevant, germane, or material to YOUR existence. Simplify that which is complex, eliminate that which is superfluous, and for God's sake, know the difference between the two. Stop now and write down YOUR PLAN. All goals need a roadmap and time deadlines. **Once written, start moving.**

WHAT YOU MUST RETAIN FROM YOUR EUREKA EDUCATION

SECRET: Do not read each word: train your eyes to read phrases. When skimming, read one sentence of each paragraph. Usually it is the topic sentence which contains the essence.

Within five years, you will have forgotten 85% of what you learned; therefore, the most important purpose for college is learning the process, NOT the product. Besides learning how to logically think and solve a problem, you should remember the methods of how to analyze data, organize information in a meaningful useful sequence and apply facts to answer questions. A BA degree is only a platform from which to continue a lifelong search for answering questions that confront you. A mind is a terrible thing to waste. Now that you are "lettered", you have the tools to practice your theories and master a skill set that will conform to the labor (job) you select. Skill requirements will change over the 40 year time span of your work life, but the method of developing them will evolve slowly.

To help you remember the matrix you worked off of in 2012, I have summarized key landmarks that with further refinement on your part will build the boat and oars you use to go down the River of Life.

English – There are five basic themes: man leaving home to find something and returning home (Homer's Odyssey), man versus man, man versus nature, woman versus man, love, etc, and man's struggle to explain the unknown (religion, philosophy).

English 101 – Writer – Write short, active sentences. Use active verbs, avoid adverbs, participles. Always develop a lead sentence in a paragraph. Discipline yourself to insure the balance of the paragraph is germane to the lead sentence. Check spelling and enrich vocabulary by reading.

Political Science/History - You need to understand the genius of the American experiment. First, the separation of power between judiciary, legislative, and executive branches provides checks and balances. The second separation is between church and state. The third element was real power in the common people who created effective local, state, and finally a limited federal government. Lastly a democracy must follow the Rule of Law.

George Washington set our nation on a policy of isolation. The Monroe Doctrine kept foreign powers out of the western hemisphere. Abraham Lincoln centralized federal power and subordinated southern states' rights. Woodrow Wilson reversed George Washington's policy of isolation by our entry into World War I by the elite powers consolidating power with the private Federal Reserve Bank and the popular election of United States Senators.

Because of the commerce power, Article 1 Section 8, the expansion of technology, and movement of people, the trend toward centralization of control is occurring. The comfort of prosperity has led to a complacency that has increased efficiency but reduced participation. Debt is enslaving the people.

American foreign policy for freedom in theory was summed up in FDR's State of the Union message of January 6, 1941. 1. The first is freedom of speech and expression, everywhere in the world. 2. The second is freedom of every person to worship God in his own way everywhere in the world. 3. A third is freedom from want which translated into world terms means economic understanding which will secure for every nation a healthy, peaceful future for its inhabitants everywhere in the world. 4. The fourth freedom is freedom from fear, which translated into world terms is a worldwide reduction of armaments to such a point and in such a fashion that no nation will be in position to commit an act of aggression against their neighbors.

What we say is not what we do. The US broke the UN

charter by committing an act of aggression against Iraq without UN approval. In 1945, the UN and globalization began but FDR policies failed. While the European empires were dismantled, the West needed cheap raw material to expand their prosperity. To control prices, the West attempted to keep trade barriers low so local industry could not compete with mass produced products from industrialized countries. The Jewish seizure of the Holy Land in 1948 and 1967 distorted the US involvement in the Middle East. Third, rapid scientific advancements increased production but have NOT changed human behavior. Traditional religion resisted cultural assimilation and FDR's policy of freedom.

Art – is the use of skills and imagination in the production of things of beauty. It is man's attempt to capture an event, image, feeling or thought to enjoy again and again. At Eureka, the courses taught the skill of the crafts I cannot duplicate here—ceramics, dance, singing, acting. What you need to remember is to take time to "smell the roses": whether it is the peace garden on campus, God speaking to Adam on the Sistine Chapel ceiling, David's bulging muscles in Florence, the Winged Victory triumph at the Louvre or Christ suffering at the Prado in Madrid. You have seen all these. You have learned "how to observe" Art. You should take time to "feel" the music. Art comes in all forms, shapes and sizes. Like literature, use it to stimulate your vision, sharpen your imagination and feed your soul.

Have your painting that inspires you; I had my mother paint a reproduction of Salvador Dali's "Last Supper" to hang in my home.

Have photos, rings, necklaces, etc to comfort the soul after a set back. Mine is my wife's high school graduation picture: she is always so young, beautiful and happy is my heart. Art is life around you. Observe and your wisdom will grow.

Biology – all living things on earth are carbon based and consist of cells that divide themselves based on a DNA recipe. The energy source is glucose oxidized to create energy. Carbon dioxide is the by-product of living tissue in animals; oxygen is the product of plants. Oxygen levels are at 21%; carbon dioxide at .04 of atmosphere. These levels have varied from 15 to 35% Oxygen. High levels allow huge animals to fly and grow into dinosaurs. Plants used carbon dioxide in photosynthesis (sun radiation provides energy to transform nutrients into sugars and release oxygen as a by-product).

Animal life originally absorbed oxygen from sea water (that's why if waters are too polluted the oxygen level decreases and the fish cannot absorb enough oxygen through their gills and suffocate).

Some animals later evolved a lung system to extract oxygen from the air where it was more abundant. Darwin's theory of natural selection stated whatever organism adapted best to the changing environment survived best known as survival of the fittest. The weak grow hungry, fail to reproduce or are eaten by stronger animals or crowded out of sunlight if a plant.

Business – This is marketing and sales; knowing the difference between a want and a need. Ask what is the most cost effective way to attract customers and trigger a buying response. Create pictures and make specific claims which equate feelings in prospects that are satisfied by purchasing your product or service.

Keep it simple and speak in the other person's interest, use pictures to visualize your story and explain benefits connecting to your customer's needs. You complete this section:

Math – Besides basics you learned in grade school, know percentages, realize rate of change is more important than the change itself. Understand the Rule of 72. (7.2% interest divided into 72 takes ten years to double your money. For a 10% return: 72 divided by 10 takes 7.2 years to double your money.) Understand compound interest.

Philosophy – Static (what is good), - Utilitarianism – Develop thoughts where people understand that what they do themselves should be good in helping ALL of society.

Main belief structure wrestles with: 1) explaining why we exist, 2) how we should live and conduct oneself with other humans particularly and with the universe in general and 3) how to deal with death and the future beyond physical dying (major religions all postulate some "supreme being", "God", "Great Spirit" that created the earth. Hindus – natural American Indians – have many natural gods, while Jews, Moslems and Christian belief in "ONE God". Buddhists and Taoists have a rendezvous after life, to a heaven state of Nirvana or Ying and Yang, perfect balance.

All religions and rituals are designed to conform human conduct and organize family, tribes, villages, cultures, and nation states into acceptable peaceful co-existence. All basically function on the "Golden Rule": do unto others as you would have them do unto you. The big difference among the religions is that many of them teach the reverse of the Christian Golden Rule. Do NOT do to others what you do not want them to do to you. The basic difference between East (China) and West (Greece) is the value of human life and the responsibility of an individual for his actions. The West places higher value on human life and therefore expects greater individual responsibility. The East emphasizes collective good and lowers the value of life sanctioned by reincarnation so death is just a phase, not an end.

SECRET: *Lasting peace can only be achieved when a consensus is reached on the value of human life.*

Religion - the Jewish 10 Commandments:

I am the Lord your G-d who has taken you out of the land of Egypt.
You shall have no other gods but me.
You shall not take the name of the Lord your God in vain.
You shall remember the Sabbath and keep it Holy.
Honor your mother and father.
You shall not murder.
You shall not commit adultery.
You shall not steal.
You shall not bear false witness.
You shall not covet anything that belongs to your neighbor.

The Greek values were of prudence, justice, temperance, and courage; the Christian added faith, hope and charity to make seven cardinal virtues. Recognize the seven rituals or sacraments of baptism, first communion, confirmation into Church, confessions of sin, forgiveness (confession of sins), marriages, and Last Rites. The Christian faith is based on the Easter story of physical death of Jesus their savior and the spiritual conquest of death with the resurrection of life. Jews still wait for the Messiah. Islam has a heaven with no emphasis on a Second Coming.

The Lord's Prayer (also produced the creed used today at the 4th century Council of Nicene).

Psychology – Freud developed a theory of three levels of consciousness: superego (conscious), ego, and id (animal instincts). He believed human subconscious was controlling the desire to survive by reproduction. Therefore sexual desire influenced behavior. Pavlov's theory believed behavior is determined by habitual stimulus. Ring a bell when feeding a dog. After the habit formed, just by ringing the bell, the dog will salivate just like when he was eating. The debate on whether behavior is controlled by environment or genetic background (Nature vs. Nurture) still exists.

Abraham Maslow explained in 1943 in his theory of Human Motivation that after the basic needs of food, shelter, sex, sleep, safety and security, came belonging needs: acceptance, affection, and love. Once these are satisfied, people look for "esteem needs" such as social status, self respect and approval from others. Finally once these are met, people strive for self actualization, the yearning to find meaning in our lives, to express ourselves and leave a legacy.

Practice the Temple's five rules for living as stated in the Introduction.

SECRET: *Humans are shaped, influenced and conditioned by a thin veneer of civilization and controlled family (tribal behavior). It is tempered by education and specialized division of labor allowing more produce,* *thereby raising the standard of living. Humans are STILL animals and genetics control life and reproduction.*

Economics – Micro economy deals with day to day commercial activity. Macro deals with the BIG Picture.

1. It all boils down to studying the simple supply and demand that determines the <u>subjective</u> value humans put on goods and services. If there is a surplus of wheat, the price per bushel will drop if demand is constant. If there is a corn virus that destroyed the corn crop, then wheat will go up because animals and humans will use the surplus of wheat to replace the demand for corn. This greatly increases corn value because supplies were reduced by disease. Another example of relationship between supply and demand: in 1930, you could have made the best buggy whip product on the market but with cars taking the transportation market share from horses, aggregate demand for whips went down and the business withered, changed products or went out of business. Technology will speed up the transmission for products and services. Globalization will accelerate expedentially the development of new products. In 2012 I did my second world cruise and it was obvious that people around the world quickly accepted a new technology but not a new culture. The tension between new tools and traditional cultural values will intensify. Can humans control robots, artificial intelligence, alien vaccines or space exploration? If civilization cannot

handle the massive transformation by 2065, Isaac Newton's predictions will usher in a new "dark age".

2. Karl Marx, founder of Communism, stated capital is simply stored labor. The value of labor depends on supply and demand. Government artificially influences labor supply and value by labor laws:
   - Jones Act helped unions (minimum wage, time and a half pay after 40 hours of work per week), forbids children from working
   - Compulsive education required for certain professions and skills
   - expanded wars to destroy goods and create artificial demand for guns, weapons, transportation services, etc.
   - Stored labor value is controlled by governments to provide collective services that individuals cannot do well or not at all e.g. police, fire, army, common currency, postal services, courts, etc.

Since 1913, with the income tax constitution amendment and federal reserve banking (fracture banking rules), government has seized total control of the money supply (no gold standard), rate of accumulated money, graduated progressive income tax (wealthy pay higher percentage of income), different tax rates or earned income (labor) and capital gain (income from capital use). The Government controls value. By using the banking system, the government controls prices of goods by setting the amount of rent you pay to use someone else's money/interest.

Government protects demands disguised as safety, health, and purity with tariffs on cheaper goods produced outside of the country. Regulations, health restriction, regulated monopoly (electricity, cable, telephone) affect demands and supplies. Marketing and "education licenses" affect demand. Taxation intervention can increase supply (tax subsidy credit i.e. wind power) or reduce value by raising prices thus destroying demand i.e. carbon tax on coal.

When was your Eureka "moment"?
KNOWLEDGE YOU DID NOT GET FROM EUREKA BUT WILL NEED TO SUCCEED.

NEGOTIATING TECHNIQUES

How to Win an Argument: The best way is to avoid it in the first place. If not possible, welcome the exchange while staying calm. Control your temper and consider what the other side wants. Let the other side finish talking. Establish points you can agree upon or at least be flexible in interpreting their point of view. Know exactly what you want and try to position the parties so that both sides come out winning something. Thank the other side for their ideas, admit errors and apologize for your mistake. Let your guard down but only for a limited purpose. Never assume anything. Get as many relevant facts as possible. Win the big one and let the other side have the little ones. Finally you want action but do not move in haste. Set up another meeting next week to review progress.

Everyone is a salesman. To be successful in marketing,

you must remember the seven "P's": 1. Passion in dealing with product or service; 2. Problem-Does it solve a real problem; 3. Profitable-Can you sell or produce the service profitably? 4. Price-What is the price margin? Can it be reduced and still be profitable? 5. Prospect-What is the prospect that the product will be used by a massive audience? 6. Promise-What promise can you give to your customers that your product will sell? 7. Presentation-How will your presentation enhance the sale and use of the product?

SECRET: *When we treat man as he is, we make him worse than he is. When we treat him as if he already were what he potentially could be, you make him what he should be. Johann Wolfgang von Goethe*

When negotiating, practice writing one-page memos. Use short memos at home, work and play.

1. State the problem, issue or question in a simple statement.
2. Put down your bottom line solution or actions.
3. Support position with bullets – facts.
4. End with a specific plan of action you wanted; work within a time frame.

All the above is fine and dandy but HOW does one DO IT. Man has used variations of the following seven forces to accomplish his end. Before applying these weapons you should realize people are CONTROLLED by the following in this order of importance.

A. Money (It's what makes the world go round.)

B. Bosses-Intimidation, brute force, sexual control and job insecurity.

C. Law and government

D. Religious fear of damnation (for many, this is number one!)

E. Image (reputation among peers)

F. Relationships (unions, brotherhoods)

G. Media

How do the seven forces control and use knowledge? Here are techniques to guide your ship down the River.

Tool 1 – Force. Although primitive, it is the most effective short term weapon for results. Beating up someone and taking their money gets results (it's illegal).

Tool 2 – Fear. Many times, the fear of violence will accomplish the results without physical action. This fear can be leveraged and expanded to fear of God, fear of catching a disease, fear of failure, and fear of not being accepted by the gang are examples. Remember MAN'S PRIME MOTIVATOR IS THE AVOIDANCE OF PAIN. Fear can be used to "persuade".

Tool 3 – Guilt. Its effect depends on the facts, situations and degree of perceived PAIN. If a person is strongly spiritual, their guilt of "sins" over past acts is very effective. If they have no conception of the "afterlife", guilt is less likely to persuade.

Tool 4 – Honor, equity, duty. If there is no guilt trip, maybe you can strike a cord concerning "service". If the person is a veteran, flying a US flag, is dependent on parents, etc, you can usually disguise the "fairness doctrine" to get a favorable response.

<u>Tool 5 – Sacrifice.</u> Women are especially vulnerable to the ploy because society reinforces sacrifice for children. Government uses this all the time claiming we need to sacrifice for the needy. We must sacrifice to free the oppressed, down-trodden masses. We must accept the huddled masses yearning to be FREE.

<u>Tool 6 – Approval.</u> It is the opposite side of the fear motivator. Younger or duller people tend to be more controlled by the acute need to fit in. If the herd instinct is strong and a person is a joiner, be it a gang, 4-H, church, Lions, etc, expect the virtue of satisfying their inner desire to be approved, seek praise or recognition. Use it to get people to buy into your proposal. Once they have a stake, you have them hooked; just reel them in.

<u>Tool 7 – Image.</u> A supportive tool that refines the need for approval is image manipulation. People seeking approval want to be "better". They are unhappy with the status quo, but do not know how to escape. You show them a vision. An image of how they will look with the product or service only you can provide. I always remember the 50 year old man who came to the motel on a $40,000 motorcycle with all the bells and whistles. I asked: "Why do you own this expensive toy?" His reply: "To get the chicks who want to ride". He bought the image.

Tool 8 – <u>Misinformation</u>. Of all the tools, this is the foulest of all. Politicians and our government are increasingly using misinformation to cloud, distort, and misdirect us in understanding the problem.

Tool 9 – <u>Exile.</u> It accompanies fear but it has a special overlay. If you control the agenda, marriage, job site, car pool, bowling league, whatever, the subtle knowledge you have enhances all of the above tools. It is like a file to keep the teeth sharp, the blade clean, or the screwdriver head flat.

If you follow the Golden Rule and the four points of the Templar Cross, tools 4, 6 and 7 should be the tools of choice. Con artists and scammers depend on tools 2, 3, 5, and 8 to cheat people. Be careful. **Remember the Golden Rule.**

OCCUPATION

If you are going to be self employed, pick where you want to live and live within walking distance of your work. To succeed you need the following ingredients:

    A. For sales, you must have a competitive advantage
    B. Everything must be focused on sales

C. Develop a business that can grow without your personal involvement

D. Before starting, determine HOW MUCH YOU can lose

E. Improve strength before working on weaknesses

F. Do not diversity in the beginning

G. Let your winners run and cut your losses early

H. Remember Pareto Principle: "80% of your sales come from 20% of your clients".

Cultivate the 20%

Here are some of the popular types of businesses that have made people millions:

Vitamins and nutritional supplements (especially sport oriented), toys, tobacco, self improvement courses, pet (photo, supplies, toys) informational newsletters, jewelry and gems, do it yourself whatever, collectibles, internet, coffee, candy, electronics, beauty aids, artist supplies, tools, pens.

If you are going to be a wage slave, here are some sobering facts. In 1970 based on US government figures, the average wage for the poorest one fifth of the work force was $9,032, the richest one fifth earned $98,322 and the median income was $39,604. In 2006, the poorest one fifth earned $11,352 while the richest one fifth earned $168,700 with the median at $48,201 based upon 2006 inflation adjusted dollars. These government figures do NOT include transfer payments (food stamps, etc), nor employer paid fringe benefits that are part of pre-taxed income. No wonder America wanted change in 2008. In 36 years, the lowest fifth had a 26% earning increase, the median income wage earner had over a 22% increase, 4% worse than the bottom fifth. The top fifth had a 71% increase: the rich were (are) getting richer. A college graduate earns more but the spread has narrowed as more middle class children get college degrees.

If you do not work for yourself (my suggestion is to work for yourself), remember to have a written plan for career development in the company. However, before we can study how to improve on the job, we must get a job. Remember when preparing for a job interview, the employer is NOT interested in you. The company is interested in itself. Searching for a job is a sales job. You must sell yourself. In your resume, say something about the company. Research the product or service they provide. Know where the core business lies. At the interview, let the company talk about the company. When asked questions, focus on why you are qualified to fill the position. Explain how you can do the task required. Persuade the company that you know their business.

After the interview, make sure you send a thank you. The letter should be handwritten on nice stationary and mention the employer BY NAME. In a positive light, say something specific about the interview. Use persistence afterward until you know the position is filled.

Once you get the job, you need to work hard to keep the job. Come into work earlier than your boss. Work harder than your peers while seeking more training and cross training. Finally help your boss plan your future, making sure you are not irreplaceable. If you are, he will NOT want you to leave.

Move from being an extraordinary employee to one that is invaluable. You do this by mastering a financially valued skill that YOU can apply to the core profit center of your employer. Study how your company makes a profit, figure out how YOU contribute to that profit. Modify your job so it contributes to the profit and make sure your bosses who determine raises know how many dollars you made for the company.

If you take my advice and work for yourself, here are a few guidelines. Have a product or service you love. If you love practicing law, do it. If not, find something else that makes you happy (and you will never "work" a day in your life).

Great people make great businesses. Seek out good people to network with as well as good employees. Money makes many people make money. Grow good people; give them incentives to grow with you.

Develop systems (standard operating procedures). It increases productivity, reduces stress and lets you concentrate on the client or customer and not the product.

Have a PLAN: daily, yearly, five years. No pro forma or prospectus. Write out a <u>detailed</u> plan, have it on everyone's computer (work bench, etc). Set specific benchmarks, timelines. Make it a talking document not one collecting dust.

Have a philosophy and clean signature. Know who you are and present it truthfully to your client base. Mine was to provide the fastest, less expensive, simplest legal product. The "professionals" and judges hated me but the client who paid the bill loved me.

Getting back to the beginning: Do you enjoy the run? Make it enjoyable. If it is no longer fun, quit and find something YOU enjoy. Life is short and you will be dead a long time.

Build an emotional bank account. All lives and businesses have ups and downs. In other parts of the book I tell you to save 10-15% of earnings and build a support team and family. But your ship down the River of Life will not sail well unless you provide two other reserves. The first is the emotional bank account. Money or friends will NOT cushion the body blows you will suffer in life; (however, your support system will prove invaluable so don't shut out family and friends). Whether it is being rejected by Harvard or fame for a criminal offense, you need to have emotional resources to get over the rapids. To build the reserve, remember the following: Seek to understand the other side of why they are doing what they are doing. Clarify expectations. Cloudy expectations lead to misunderstandings, friction, conflict and ultimate PAIN. Do not doubt yourself but after reviewing reality, life may require a reassessment of the journey and a change of course.

Show personal integrity. Be honest, do not betray others' confidences. Admit your mistake, apologize sincerely, but stand your ground on principles. You must be able to live with yourself.

Keep commitments, do not make promises you can not keep. Cultivate the ability to pay attention to little kindnesses and courtesies.

The second reserve you need to build is a reserve of love and trust with your spouse, significant other, sibling, friend, etc. The key to building an emotional reserve with your spouse is DO NOT GET INTO POWER PLAYS. Communicate. Together work out a financial, emotional, sexual, and physical arrangement that both parties realistically can achieve. Like the business plan, explained before, have a daily, yearly, five year plan posted in the house. Review it, talk about it, plan together and work together. Draw off of each others strengths, complement their weaknesses and DO NOT SWEAT the little things. If there are children, bring them into the planning and execution as early as possible. Hold them accountable. Review and refresh marriage vows. Center on love and commitment. Keep your eyes downstream as you cannot go back, so forgive and do not rehash the past. Do not stand up and try to jump ship for another mate; you could drown.

ENTREPRENEUR

You will only advance financially by either money earning more money OR having people work for you and you make money from their labor.

You should ALWAYS invest in yourself by learning by observation, from formal education and learning new marketable skills.

You should use other people by going into business. To be successful, you MUST be able to manage competition, shareholders, clients, potential clients, employees, taxes, and regulations. If you cannot handle those challenges, then explore what educational skills you can develop to live and save to have money make you money under the investment section of this book. If you decide business is the path to independence, here are the factors to succeed.

- Do market research; study the competition, and the locations, needs and desires test.
- Make sure there is a need for your product or service.
- Death, Debt, and Divorce: these allow you to buy a franchise or business.
- Do not incorporate until you have a going business then use a C Corp in Delaware or Wyoming.
- Build your product first, and then raise money. You need a service or product people need NOW.
- If not technical, use a founder to develop product; if absolutely necessary outsource when needed.
- Make sure all founders invest money into the business.
- Manage company, handle ideas, bring in revenues, and build a product or service.
- Get customs first, then patent later.
- No need for non-compete agreement; no one will steal your idea.
- Listen to venture capitalists but do NOT do what they want; you need to do it yourself.
- Over deliver in the first 100 days.
- Say no to obvious losses, sell, sell, cut costs: focus only after success of product or service.
- If no business after two (2) months, give up and move on.
- Admit mistakes: work with clients like a partner to solve problems.
- Stay local first; expand only after local success.
- Hire a professional to do applications if business warrants computers.
- Blog and become the voice of your industry.

- Hire people only after getting revenue, no office.
- Do not quit job until you have six (6) months reserve to cover expenses.
- Advisors are useless and a waste of money; YOU know your business best.
- Ideas are hard; execution is the key to success.
- Do not use a Public Relations firm: too expensive
- No bartering; get cash.
- Release fast, with new features every week; repackage, promote the future.
- The best clients are old clients. Go back to your client to sell others your product or service.
- When rejected, contact client once a month. Never get angry.
- Never gossip. Do NOT talk badly about a partner or investor of your business.
- Do not give raises to employees; use gifts, incentives, praise and perks.
- Give 15-20% in employee options: in bonuses, IRA, parking, coupons, childcare, etc.
- Use email: highly targeted marketing written by professional copywriters.
- Send Christmas gift baskets, birthday cards, thank you cards and have a suggestion box.
- Maybe give out free stuff (only 3% of "free" customers turn into paying customers)
- Pay no taxes; reinvest profits into the business and hard assets supporting the business.

You need to incorporate the factors into a written business

plan. Be realistic on costs, conservative on revenue. Once the need and test prove successful, prepare to launch. Preparation is vital. DO NOT launch until the finances are secure, product is available, and the need is established. If any one of these is deficient, you will FAIL. Better to abandon an idea and find another opportunity from the Death, Debt, Divorce bargains. Once found, prepare business roadmap on how you are going to execute. Business is tough and if you cannot manage the issues outlined in the first paragraph, DO NOT try. Invest in yourself and make money to make money.

Now you have decided to be an entrepreneur, what tactics will support your business?

- Must be GOAL oriented, short, one (1) year, vision of the future (long term)
- All parties MUST be positively motivated daily; promote health
- No room for negative attitudes; turn lemons into lemonade
- Fidelity is vital; each day will have its challenges. Teamwork/network will assist in getting the job done.
- Determination, no excuses, whining or putting off until tomorrow. A good roadmap to finish helps, PLAN, PLAN, PLAN.
- As the leader, founder, president, you have to project confidence both internally to employees, partners, etc and externally to clients, the competition, bankers, investors, etc. Without confidence, there is NO trust. People must trust you and your product/service before they buy it.

- Self-discipline is essential; be tough on yourself. Set up Standard Operating Procedures (SOP). Make sure everyone understands them and ACT on the mission statement. Be fair but tough; set a good example for everyone. Do not tolerate gossip or fake news.
- Build consensus if possible; the spirit of growth, fulfillment of needs: success.
- Emulate the posture of your customers; it's their problem or need you are satisfying. Look behind what they say.
- By doing all of the above, trust will be established. With trust, you can expand service and profit with less expense.
- Design product or service as to hold attention: by teasing, suggesting new items, redesigning or repackaging old items.
- Use expensive looking business card, thank you cards and website. Dress and act like you already have it made. Finally, ACT, do not just DREAM! employed and managing a business where money and employees create profits for you. Do not fall into the trap that a business is simply replacing your income from a job.

Remember with a job, you have regular income (paycheck), IRA or 401K benefits, vacation time, sick leave, insurance possibly employer funded, conferences, education expenses, possibly maternity or family leave, disability and/or unemployment benefits, long term services, bonuses, possibly car use or transportation/parking subsidy. Balance the benefits plus working 40 hours a week with self-employment or a business where it will be a 24-hour 7-day (24/7) commitment to succeed.

Review the steps outlined on starting a business. I cannot emphasize enough that most failures result from

- A lack of immediate need for the product or service
- A failure to test and structure a realistic written business plan
- A failure to have enough money to survive the first year of operation. The amount and cost of money generally kills the business plan. Don't be fearful of failure. If you refuse to try new things, you will end life with "I could have", "I might have" or "I should have". Your life will be a path to Hell.

You are unique. Focus on being the best person YOU CAN BE. Being envious of others is negative energy. LIFE IS NOT FAIR. Your characteristics make you what you are. If you are a 5'2" boy then being a professional basketball player is probably not the best career choice. Money does not define your legacy. It is merely a resource to use. Your ability to analyze your talents, your passions and your resources provide you the drive to a self-fulfilling and productive life, a true legacy.

To help in selecting the path away from hell, the following will augment your discovery of yourself.

- Invest in yourself. Every day seek ways to GROW. Before you speak, listen carefully.

- Before you ACT, think of the known and unknown consequences of your choices.
- Before you spend thousands on college or seminars, etc., determine what you will learn from the time and money spent.
- Before you invest your time and money in a new job, self-employment or a business, investigate ALL of the benefits and drawbacks of your actions.
- Before you criticize, put yourself in the shoes of the people on the other side of the issue. Maybe you are too greedy, maybe the big print is great, but the details restrict growth and progress. Maybe you need more advice or data before criticizing.
- Develop saving habits early and with the magic of compound interest, work forward.
- Organize your insurances, emergency reserves, debt level and quality of products and services used to reduce stress which disturbs your sleep at night.

Finally, have a Plan B and an emergency Plan C (family?) back up. If after acting with perseverance and you fail, you can pick yourself up and correct the course of direction to avoid hell on earth.

In order to know where you are, you must have a realistic WRITTEN BUDGET. Now you can analyze where you are going, what needs to be reduced to create an emergency fund and SAVE. Always spend less than you take in. There are many bill organizers that you can download off the internet. Find one that works for you and your expenses. Then use it!

WHY NOT TO BE AN ENTREPRENEUR

You need to evaluate your temperament and ability to handle the issues of running a business. There is an enormous sense of achievement (not to mention wealth) in creating and building a successful enterprise. Remember only money and making money from other people's labor creates wealth. There is a big difference in being self-employed and managing a business where money and employees create profits for you. Do not fall into the trap that a business is simply replacing your income from a job.

Remember with a job, you have regular income (paycheck), IRA or 401K benefits, vacation time, sick leave, insurance possibly employer funded, conferences, education expenses, possibly maternity or family leave, disability and/or unemployment benefits, long term services, bonuses, possibly car use or transportation/parking subsidy. Balance the benefits plus working 40 hours a week with self-employment or a business where it will be a 24 hour 7 day (24/7) commitment to succeed.

Review the steps outlined on starting a business. I cannot emphasize enough that most failures result from

- A lack of immediate need for the product or service
- A failure to test and structure a realistic written business plan
- A failure to have enough money to survive the first year of operation. The amount and cost of money generally kills the business plan.

Don't be fearful of failure. If you refuse to try new things, you will end life with "I could have", "I might have" or "I should have". Your life will be a path to Hell.

You are unique. Focus on being the best person YOU CAN BE. Being envious of others is negative energy. LIFE IS NOT FAIR. Your characteristics make you what you are. If you are a 5'2" boy then being a professional basketball player is probably not the best career choice. Money does not define your legacy. It is merely a resource to use. Your ability to analyze your talents, your passions and your resources provide you the drive to a self fulfilling and productive life; a true legacy.

To help in selecting the path away from hell, the following will augment your discovery of yourself.

- Invest in yourself. Every day seek ways to GROW. Before you speak, listen carefully.
- Before you ACT, think of the known and unknown consequences of your choices.
- Before you spend thousands on college or seminars, etc, determine what you will learn from the time and money spent.
- Before you invest your time and money in a new job, self employment or a business, investigate ALL of the benefits and drawbacks of your actions.
- Before you criticize, put yourself in the shoes of the people on the other side of the issue. Maybe you are too greedy, maybe the big print is great but the details restrict growth and progress. Maybe you need more advice or data before criticizing.
- Develop saving habits early and with the magic of compound interest, work forward.

– Organize your insurances, emergency reserves, debt level and quality of products and services used to reduce stress which disturbs your sleep at night.

Finally, have a Plan B and an emergency Plan C (family?) back up. If after acting with perseverance and you fail, you can pick yourself up and correct the course of direction to avoid hell on earth.

In order to know where you are, you must have a realistic WRITTEN BUDGET. Now you can analyze where you are going, what needs to be reduced to create an emergency fund and SAVE. Always spend less than you take in. There are many bill organizers that you can download off the internet. Find one that works for you and your expenses. Then use it!

INVESTING

Excellence is not an act, but a habit. -- Aristotle

I could write a whole book on saving and investing but since there are volumes out there, I will simply recite a few pillars of knowledge to apply to all savings and investing.

1. If the investment sounds too good to be true, it is.
2. Don't fight the Federal Reserve interest rate.

If interest rates are going up and the federal bank is restricting the economy, stay out of common stocks. If interest rates are going down and the Federal Reserve is stimulating the economy, buy stocks. If long term bond rates are lower than low term rates, a recession is coming.

3. Don't fall in love with a stock; it won't fall in love with you.
4. Do not put more than 5% at risk in any one investment.
5. The trend is your friend until the end. Follow moving averages. When five days goes above a 29-day averages, buy; when there is a five day drop below the 29-day average-sell.
6. Invest in businesses you understand that pay <u>dividends</u> from <u>growing</u> profits.
7. Buying at a low price is key to value: real estate, stocks; and/or a collection/hobby you enjoy such as coins or art.
8. Care about risk more than returns. Use moving stop losses to adjust the % from 20% depending on the volatility ranges of stock.
9. It takes courage to be a pig: cut your losses and let your profit ride.
10. Learn from your mistakes, have patience, study, seek free advice from Vanguard or other reputable services.
11. Eight out of ten mutual funds do NOT do better than an ETF index fund.
12. Avoid waste killers: TV, web browsing, arguments, trying to be number one, worrying about things you cannot change.

13. Buy real estate: for example, if a person age 22 with a $30,000 a year job takes 7.5% of his income that gives 4% annually and invests in real estate with a 30% return of investment he will have an $18,000,000 real estate portfolio by age 50. Enough to retire on.

14. Buy real estate right: look for vacant homes or apartments, watch garage sales (often they occur before one moves), establish contacts with nursing homes and attorneys (they have information on who got sick and are moving out of their homes). Only after expansion buy farm land, then commercial, forest, or industrial.

15. Do not buy insurance as an investment. *Compounding Interest is the Eighth Wonder of the World -- Use it to expand wealth.*

16. The health care business is changing fast. The tax laws have provided some advantages for Flexible Spending Accounts (FSA) and Health Savings Accounts (HSA). If you are healthy, secure a high deductible insurance plan, and set aside up to $6900 tax deductible in a (HSA) account. The money in the plan can be invested and earn income and will never be taxed as long as it is eventually used for health expenses.

17. Avoid short term capital gains which are taxed at ordinary income. As long as a stock is held for one year or more, it will be taxed at 0-15% while short term gains will be taxed at 10-35%.

18. Make the most of your affiliations, political and military unions, become a regular customer and ask for VIP discount always.

19. Buy a fixer-up home. Buy the cheapest home in an expensive area, live in it for two years or more, fix it up. Then sell it. All gains up to $125000 per person are tax free.

The stock market is rigged to support the elite. When investing, watch for these red flags:

1) Pump and dump-promoters will promote a stock and then quickly dump it. Prices go down much faster than they go up.

2) Poop and scoop- opposite of Pump and dump.

3) Stop hunting-Insiders watch where retail investors place a stop level to get out of if the stop goes down to that limit. Stock manipulators will sell a stock to push it down below the stop limit and then quickly buy calls above the limits to make a profit.

4) Spoofing- The elites will create the appearance of massive amounts of orders that are not genuine and quickly evaporate on a stock movement, causing panic.

5) Newsletters and brokers will front-run a stock. They buy it up first, then later promote it in their newsletter as a great buy.

6) Big institutions and billionaires use dark pool trading to sell stocks outside of the public exchanges so that retail investors do not know who actually owns the securities.

7) Companies will purposely release false stories to push the stock price up or down artificially. Remember 80% of the market is owned by institutions and retail

traders only consist 15% of the market regardless of what Acorn or Robinhood says.

In closing here is a short list of stable stocks that pay dividends. Make sure you sell covered calls to add to your income. GSK, MSFT, LLY, MDT, CVS, ABBV, JNJ, WFC, KO, MMM, DIS, MSD, CVX, CL, TGT, and HRL.

TAXES

SECRET: *Taxation in reality is life. If you know the position a person takes on taxes, you can tell their whole philosophy.*

The law changes so much, there is no way I can guide on specific moves. Congress constantly changes the rules to provide full time employment for the tax service industries, CPAs, tax lawyers and lobbyist so they in turn will channel funds into their campaigns. Until we have a flat tax and a national sales tax, the basic game will not change.

Since 1913, when the graduated Income Tax movement took hold, the wealthy shifted taxation away from WEALTH to income. Because of this philosophy, the wealthy do not pay a fair share of the taxes. Remember these principles when pushing the oars.

1. Try not to realize income. The rich go not sell real assets. They use 1031 exchange. Without sales and the use of trusts, wealth is used and preserved. Remember the IRS only taxes income, not wealth.

2. If you have to realize income, try not to recognize it. Life insurance, municipal bonds and mineral depletion allowance are examples of ways to avoid federal tax on realized income. Employers pay fringe benefits, i.e. health insurance, lunch room, gym, etc.

3. Try to convert ordinary income into capital gains.

4. If you cannot capitalize, then defer recognition. Pension funds, annuities, options and deferred compensation packages are the favorites. EVERYONE SHOULD HAVE AN IRA, ROTH 401 plan and max out employers plans. The wealthy use Code 1031 to "exchange" like-kind property, and then do not pay taxes on the exchange.

5. If there is no other way, split the income to reduce the tax bracket you are in. The kiddie tax stopped the practice for the middle class. Children earned income is exempt. Corporations and trusts can be used by the rich. Put children to work in family businesses. You pay NO social security taxes on children income.

Plan ahead. Besides income taxes, do not forget all the other taxes. Buy on the internet to avoid sale taxes, buy at garage sales, used items from private parties. Appeal your real estate taxes and if you have a choice, look at state and local taxes when picking a place to live. If you practice the lessons in life section, you already are avoiding the sin taxes on tobacco, alcohol, gambling, etc. It always feels good to let someone else pay the bill.

You're already ahead of the game if you follow the advice on wealth building. By keeping <u>good</u> records and using the techniques in starting your own business, you are using <u>before</u> tax dollars. Store value of wealth whether it be a forest project, coins, a hobby. Find a passion and let the government subsidize it. The wealthy use private foundations to get government to subsidize their charitable giving. You are subsidizing Yale and Harvard endowments to let the rich get richer.

SECRET: "There are two ways not to suffer from poverty. The first is acquire more wealth. The second is to limit your requirements. The first is not always in our power. The second is."-Tolstoy. Calendar of Wisdom, 1912.

RETIREMENT OUTLINE FOR AGES 30 AND UNDER

A. Start early with a written life plan, 1 year, 5 year and life.
B. You can split the annual $6000 contribution with a Roth IRA that is not tax deductible when originally put in. The Roth grows and there I no income tax when withdrawn after age 591/2. I suggest $3000 deposited in a traditional IRA and $3000 in a Roth IRA every year. Borrow if you must because you cannot go back and put money in for prior years.
C. Study your 401K options. Consider the employee benefits and not the raw salary when taking a job or career path.

D. Save an emergency fund of 6 months of your salary in order to cover the black swans of life-house repairs, appliance breakdown and car repairs. Then work on a vacation savings fund so that you do not have to use credit cards so that you can enjoy the annual vacation.

E. Analyze and understand the difference between good debt and bad debt. Good is your house, business or tools; bad is credit card debt.

SAVING TIPS

Here are tips – valid in 2010. Marketing constantly changes so check for new information.

- Always have an emergency fund so you DO NOT PAY credit card interest.
- Ask, ask, ask for discounts, rebates, match web offers, promotional groups, loyalty cards.
- Barter or trade one item for another and expand expertise (woodworking, sewing).
- Buy used. Use Auction sites.
- Credit Cards: get best benefits that you will use, i.e. Citicard now offers 2% on everything, others offer 5% discount on gas, air miles, etc.

– Craigslist.com: free website to buy and sell items (beware!!!)
– Dentist: use dental schools. Compare prices, use specialty shops for dentures.
– Electricity: get Power Company to do an energy audit. Know where your electricity is being used. Pull the plugs for energy savings (phone rechargers use energy, unplug.) Use fans, LED lights, electric heater in one living room (house thermostat can be turned down), wear sweaters and turn down heat. Use humidifier in winter to add moisture to the air; use a dehumidifier in summer to cut down the air conditioners job.
– FBR: Floss daily before bed, Brush your teeth carefully with soft brush for two minutes, Rinse to kill bacteria and freshen breath. Every morning, scrape your tongue to remove bacteria and toxins from being swallowed and being reabsorbed back into the body.
– Insurance: use high deductible. If car is over six years old, buy liability only.
– Library: use it for books, movies, art, computers, etc. Make use of museums, schools, parks.
– Live near work. Do you really need a car or can you use Uber/Lyft, the bus, or ride share.
– Make double mortgage payments: use Credit Unions.
– Negotiate with CASH: negotiate everything, health care, dentist
– Phone: check out internet providers. Shop carefully! Do you still need a home phone?
– Plant a garden

- Rest: use blue or green for décor, an eyeshade for light pollution, silence (sound blockers, earplugs, FM radio or static for white noise generator, keep humidity at 60-70%, buy the best mattress you can afford, rotate your mattress every three months, buy Egyptian cotton, bamboo or silk bedding and bedclothes, turn clock away so you don't watch it, read until drowsy. Be sure to keep cell phones at least three feet away from your bed, or better yet, in the next room. Stop looking at screens at least one hour before bed. Have a consistent routine.
- Storage: Keep drugs and food in cool, dry, dark place. Buy in bulk or on sale and stock up.
- Secondhand: Try to buy from estate sales or garage sales in wealthy part of the city.
- Second Opinion: always try to get a second quote for operations or work.
- Travel: check out several websites including the hotel's own site. AAA may NOT be the best price. Read the fine print to know cancellation penalties. Periodically, recheck the price; if the price has gone down and if there are NO penalties, go ahead and cancel and rebook. BE CAREFUL. Read the fine print.
- Travel: use the internet to book cruises and air either way in advance or last minute. After negotiating the best deal with whomever, bid 20% less on Priceline to see if you can get even more savings. Remember the Best Deal has no cancellation or insurance so you are committed. Understand completely what you are getting. Scams are everywhere.

- Vinegar: use for cleaning windows, toilets, sinks. Vinegar can be used as a health aide for colds, bad breath, upset stomach (natural apple cider vinegar with the mother is the best).
- Walk: it is free exercise and saves gas. Use a bicycle or scooter.
- Warehouse coupon network clubs: BJ's, Costco and Sam's can save you money if you can use bulk amounts. Check local stores for items on sale for smaller quantities; wait for the sales.
- Get free information from publications.USA. gov17192952675. Medicare information 877-267-2323 Places to get low medical costs through medical tourisim-404-373-8282. Reduce drug costs 800-712-1213; Reduce hearing aid costs 866-956-5400, ext 2; Go to Amazon warehouse or outlet for further bargains.

Lastly ask, ask, ask, for children or senior discounts.

SECRET: *A penny saved is a penny earned without income taxes.*

Everyone says save but most people do not. Until now I was always an advocate of saving but with the radical changing dollar, I have to review my premise. Since I was in high school in 1968, the purchase power of a dollar has eroded 75%. A dollar today purchases what a quarter will now. Assuming I saved $1 in 1974 when I started to work and earned 6% per annum after taxes. Using the rule of 72, I divide 72 by 6 to equal 12 years. My money doubled every 12 years. That means my $1 equaled $2 in 1986, it equaled $4 in 1998 and it equaled $8 in 2010. Unfortunately my $8 purchase power is cut by 75% meaning I can only receive about $2 in 1974 values. A double in 36 years is not a big incentive. Because of the inflation and devaluation for the average person I suggest the following:

1. If you are planning on staying at your present location for more than five years, seriously consider buying your home. The interest and real tax deductions provide an incentive to own rather than rent.

2. Maximize your retirement plan because income taxes are deferred on the appreciation. You will not be tempted to use your money on consumption now.

3. DO NOT use consumer debt, rent to own, deferred furniture plans etc. SAVE up money at your local non-profit credit union until you have the CASH to buy what you want/need. Same goes for automobiles and vacations. Unless a dependable vehicle is a MUST to hold your job, car pool or use public transportation, buy an older vehicle before borrowing for a car.

The culture of America has changed over the last century. In 1900, about 25% of the people saving were in real estate and consumer durables, about 27% went into stocks and bonds, 34% into unincorporated businesses (farms, local business) and 3% in pensions and life insurance. Today 45% is in real estate, 35% in stocks and bonds, 15% in pensions and life insurance and only 7% in self employed businesses. Instead of running your own business, we now are slaves to corporate business. Workers are happy but nonetheless NOT independent. We have tried to buy security with putting more into real estate and pensions.

This is really NOT true, because banks and government have made credit easy so more could purchase houses. Easy credit increases demand and we have an artificial high value on housing. Many people are slaves to their mortgage payments. Excesses caused defaults.

Are you NOT contradicting what you just advised about buying a home? No, home buying is a good policy, but remember you need to bargain hunt, as long as it fits your needs. Keep your needs <u>small</u> and <u>diversify</u> money into other investment vehicles.

In closing, keep your needs small and save.

SECRET: *The definition of class: The longer you can postpone gratification of a current passion, the higher class you are. Remember the Greeks: Practice moderation in all things, including moderation.*

How do you save? Write down ALL expenditures. Use the computer to compare cost. ASK: do I really need this? Buy used. (Depends on the item!!!) Don't worry about the Jones's. Save up and then buy "it". SAVE for particular goals: house, vacation, college, etc. Reward the family for saving. Read section on Taxes and do not be talked into insurance. Get insurance if you need insurance but remember it is NOT an investment.

SKILLS

Persistence is the twin sister of excellence. One is a matter of quality; the other, a matter of time." Marabel Morgan

Skills are less important than health, wisdom and knowledge. Skills are job specific and will need to be mastered to complete your specific job description. The following are work place skills that apply to all jobs.

Remember the pyramid at the beginning. We built the foundation of health, wisdom, knowledge and now skills. Alas, human nature is weak. For most people, if I offer them a $100 or these words of wisdom, the wealth seeker would take the money. Unfortunately, they ignore the wisdom and waste the money, leaving them adrift.

Be the exception, go back and reread the entire book and take notes this time. Before we start, you need to understand how STRESS can destroy all your efforts in learning and using your skill to help others.

For example: A leader, when explaining stress management to his class, raised a glass of water and asked: "How heavy is this glass of water?"

Answers called out ranged from 4 to 16 ounces.

The leader replied, "The absolute weight doesn't matter. It depends on how long you try to hold it. If I hold it for a minute, that's no sweat. If I hold it for an hour, I'll have an ache in my right arm. If I hold it for a day, it will get heavier and heavier. Pain will consume my attention. Finally I will collapse, the glass will break and I will have failed.

The above story illustrates why everyday stress is much more damaging than crises (death of a spouse, child, or loss of your job). Daily stress wears you down, speeds the heart rate, dilates the pupils, and floods the blood with painful and damaging hormones.

Stress has more to do with your psychological makeup than your immediate surroundings. It's all in your mind.

Aids:

1. Avoid catastrophic thinking (don't overstate reality)
2. Avoid absolutist thinking: I must, I should, I ought. This leads to unnecessary frustration. (Remember you have no direct control of others.)
3. Meditation (prayer). Use the beads. Practice progressive relaxation (alternate tensing then relaxing each body group.).
4. Develop fantasies. Adopt three to six alternative states of mind focusing on relaxation themes (example: use handkerchief to wipe your face or clean your glasses thinking about the great 30 foot jump you made to win the high school championship). Hold your breath and move your arms as you come up out of the water saving a beautiful (girl or boy) from the Rock River. Bend over and touch your knees as you carefully set down a heavy load of wood you broke off the ice, carry it from the windy cold porch walking back into the room

with a warm potbelly stove. A family experience will do. Remember it must have body action, be rewarding and pleasant. (some women touch their breast and feel a baby suckling). It's important to make sure you change your breathing; deeply held breaths work best for most people.

Second take vacations, eat right, exercise regularly and utilize proper sleep patterns. On your vacation, do long and short trips. Plan the trip 20 times in your brain: it will reduce stress. Keep reminders of past trips to divert one's mind when frustrated to pleasant thoughts of your favorite experiences.

Once you understand how stress affects you, make sure you take care of yourself. Study the simple yet essential. Learn to cook because you know what actual foods you are eating. Provide safe clean shelter. Use plants to filter the air. Select a residence where you have sunshine, fresh clean air (no chemicals). Make sure you have SAFE WATER for drinking but also for cleaning and washing.

Appearance and clothing are important. Dress for success. Watch personal grooming. Use natural fibers as they breathe. If you can afford it, use Egyptian cotton and silk. Have a comfortable bed. Have a firm mattress, pillow of full density to keep the head up and to relieve pressure on the spine. Try to sleep on your back or side; never sleep on your belly as it creates mechanical stress to the cervical spine. Have bright light colors in your home. If you are the nervous type, then go to earth tones. Smile occasionally, keep blinking, and nod in agreement when talking to others.

Whether you work for others or for yourself, the following skills are needed for any job.

WORK PLACE SKILLS

First cultivate relationships with workers who can teach you skills you do not have. Try to position yourself so that others depend on you. Be in a position where you are not just doing common work where anyone could displace you. On the other hand, do not become so irreplaceable that your supervisor will not promote you because no one can do your job.

While on the job, place yourself in the center of activity. Remember the golden rule while building a reputation for integrity, graciousness, goodwill and knowledge. Try not to exaggerate your worth. At the same time, use cunning and craft to control the aspects of your job that are important to your boss and satisfying to your self respect.

On a day to day basis, be approachable, positive, and practical. Inject humor while not acting like a jester. Constantly work to build a team approach toward a Goal while not vacillating in your directive, nor rehashing the past (good or bad). Always leave something on the table while keeping expectations alive for a better outcome in the future.

Look for the goodness in everything while understanding the short comings of those around you. Always act as if others are watching you. Be careful about expressing your opinions and do not be the first to state a conclusion.

Study being a judge of character. Choose a few friends carefully and cultivate those relationships realistically.

When developing relationships with others, listen carefully to what they say. Stay close to the producers, drop the losers. Listen to their intentions. The probability of results is as follows: 100% - I did, 90% - I will, 80% - I can, 70% - I think I can, 60% - I might, 50% - I think I might, 40% - What is it?, 30% - I wish I could, 20% - I don't remember how, 10% - I can't 0% - I won't. – Use your time and convert the 50% plus to "I did!"

Rely on yourself and trust your heart. Always keep something in reserve. Life is a river that is constantly flowing. Learn to go with the flow and enjoy the ride. Living the "fast life" will lead to resistance and burn out. Take a few minutes every day to do your massage, exercise and eat "good" food. A good exercise is the "Surya Namaskar" or Salutation to the Sun.

Do not carry fools on your back. While giving sincere praise, use your influence, consolation to advance the common good. While being expressive, do not get yourself into situations where you embarrass yourself or others.

Keep your eyes open, do not explain too much, and keep the mystery of your success to yourself. Always have a plan working: Option A, or B, envisioning Plan "C".

Come to work early and leave late. Always be prepared to expect the unexpected.

Feed the soul. Find your song that you can sing when alone and depressed; mine is "The Impossible Dream" composed by

Mitch Leigh with lyrics written by Joe Darion and featured in the 1965 Broadway musical Man of La Mancha:

TO DREAM THE IMPOSSIBLE DREAM
TO FIGHT THE IMPOSSIBLE FOE,
TO BEAR WITH UNBEARABLE SORROW
TO RUN WHERE THE BRAVE DARE NOT GO"

SUMMARY

Success in your career can be distilled into five guideposts. First know your competencies. Hopefully in school, you had truly analyzed your abilities and studied what comes naturally. If the best you can do is D+ in Spanish, then you best not be an interpreter. If you are 5'4", being a professional basketball player is probably out. You must be able to contribute to the company profits. Constantly read and study. If you cannot win the race by running, change your skill sets and find a passion you enjoy and be the best. Second, work with your boss. Find out what your boss wants and develop a novel method that will let both you and your boss get the credit for developing. Third, build relationships that increase your visibility. Play on a company softball team, put up art, or produce a weekly internal memo. Do extras to expand relationships. Fourth: study the firm culture. If the IBM "blue suit" culture is not for you, maybe you should look for a culture like Google where you can bring your dog to work. Do not try to change cultures: it is too hard. It's better to move on. Fifth, get business savvy. Try to talk to competitors, read trade journals, read business books for free at the library. Know where your industry was and will be. In 1924, workers for a buggy whip manufacturer were not using those skills.

Theory and rules are great but how do you apply them? One starts with a manageable job. To be successful, you need to know where you are, what needs to be done to get where your boss wants to be. Have goals. If you produce bolts, establish a production schedule that will produce x bolts per hour. Establish input and output, know the production schedule and exactly how you fit into the final output. If short term goals are not met, analyze with your boss why and who is accountable. If you make a mistake, learn from it, admit it and remedy it while moving forward. As Theodore Roosevelt said: "Do what you can, with what you have, where you are".

Second, understand primary goals in addition to your other goal you set in the preceding paragraph. What does your end user want/need? Make sure you understand the big picture otherwise your personal job tasks and goals will be frustrated and stressful.

Third, set definite deadlines and start work immediately. Postponing action loses time and money.

Fourth, communicate with your boss. If you are self-employed, then every client is your boss. Depending on culture and organization, the process will differ. Ask for frequent feedback; get written (email) evaluations to build your career profile.

Fifth, review details carefully. A minute detail could ruin the project. While getting all the details covered, you set yourself up as a can do producer in the organization.

Keep this work for reference here and a few rejoinders I have copied to use at times to spice up colorful conversation:

I thought that I could love no other, until, that is, I met your brother.

I feel so miserable without you, it's almost like having you here (Stephen Bishop)

I've had a perfectly wonderful evening. But this wasn't it. (Groucho Marx)

He is not only dull himself, he is the cause of dullness in others. (Samuel Johnson)

A modest little person, with much to be modest about. (in reference to Winston Churchill)

I've just learned about his illness. Let's hope it's nothing trivial. (Steven Cobb)

Persistence is the twin sister of excellence. One is the matter of quality; the other, a matter of time. (Marabel Morgan)

If you want it done, do it yourself.

If it is going to be, it is up to me. (Army)

Roses are red, violets are blue, sugar is sweet, and so are you. But the roses are wilting, the violets are dead, the sugar bowl is empty, and so is your head.

I love your smile, your face, and your eyes; damn, I'm good at telling lies!

My darling, my lover, my beautiful wife: Marrying you has screwed up my life.

My love, you take my breath away, what have you stepped into that smells this way?

In Vino Veritas - In Cervesio Felicitas. ("In wine, there is wisdom, in beer, there is joy.")

May the best day of your past be the worst day of your future.

May you live as long as you want, and never want as long as you live.

It is a riddle wrapped in a mystery inside an enigma.

In all this world, why I do think
There are four reasons why we drink:
Good friends, good wine, lest we be dry,
And any other reason why.

Here's to cheating, stealing, fighting, and drinking.
If you cheat, may you cheat death.
If you steal, may you steal a woman's heart.
If you fight, may you fight for a brother.
And if you drink, may you drink with me.

Dance as if no one were watching,
Sing as if no one were listening,
And live every day as if it were your last.

BULLETS TO REMEMBER and other Nuggets

A. Drink a glass of water after a meal to balance Ph factor.
B. Chew food slowly and completely; consume less and enjoy more.
C. Smile and see the glass half full not half empty.

D. Shake hands using your senses: touch, smell, sight, and hearing.

E. Pray or use biofeedback to balance life forces, boost confidence, and reduce stress.

F. Always carry aspirin; chew and swallow if you suspect heart attack or stroke

G. Keep needs small; saving is easier than earning…NO TAXES

H. Remember most prescription drugs are poisons alien to your body – follow doctor's orders

I. Use massages, press meridian points on face and feet and do practical exercises to stay healthy.

J. Observance is the window to Wisdom. Reading is the vehicle for knowledge.

K. We are animals; we communicate not just by talking. Reproduction "sex" controls "id".

L. Never forget the secret of life and the code of living.

M. Work Plan A, visualize Plan B and get family to buy into emergency Plan C.

N. Those who ignore history are condemned to repeat it.

O. Know how to use inductive and deductive reasoning to find solutions.

P. Master two skills you can sell to others.

Q. KISS: Keep it simple, stupid. Life is too short to complicate matters.

R. Don't give up.

S. Write out a Plan: Act on it by taking the first step. A journey of a thousand miles starts with a single step.

T. Secret to success is not attitude but action. The defense of the empire depends on a single grain of rice.

U. Know thyself: test your talents, guard your weaknesses. Only you can find skills to master.

V. Take the high road choice between Gold and Wisdom: choose Wisdom.

W. Know how to read map and charts. Follow your own map to goals.

X. Avoid the Plague (seven deadly sins: pride, lust, gluttony, anger, envy, greed, sloth). Practice the seven heavenly virtues: faith, hope, charity, fortitude, justice, temperance, prudence.

Y. Know your priorities: remember the pyramid; understand motivation.

Z. You are the Captain of the Ship, the Master of your Soul: Still Waters Run Deep.

Everyone lives by selling something.

Small business success is to buy low, sell high and satisfy the customer needs.

You don't get what you deserve, you get what you negotiate.

Negotiation is about compromise, not winning.

The second half of a man's life is made up of nothing but the habits he has acquired during the first half.

Always do business with a man who reads. –Andrew Carnegie

When there's nothing to lose and much to gain by trying, try. – W. Clement Stone

In my factory, we make cosmetics; but in my stores, we sell hope. – Charles Revlon

Eat not to dullness, drink not to elevation.

Ben Franklin kept a little book to record thoughts, ideas,

names and appointments, remember to do and not to do things and other important addition to his book. He made a daily chart and crossed off daily what he did in each virtue to improve his quality of life. It is important to remember Franklin started with one virtue to practice on. Only after he was confident the virtue was ingrained AS A HABIT, did he move on to improve the next.

His order of precepts was as follows:

1. TEMPERANCE – Eat not to dullness; drink not to drunkenness.
2. Silence -- talk only when the benefit is more valuable than silence.
3. Order – Timing is everything. Sharpen when is the right time to talk, work, eat, sleep, etc. Develop a rhythm that maximizes energy consumption.
4. Resolution – Do what you say you are going to do. Only promise what you can perform. Under promise, over perform.
5. Frugality – waste nothing
6. Industry – Always be doing or planning your next move
7. Sincerity – Act openly, avoid hurting others
8. Justice – Do not wrong anyone; error on the side of no action than the wrong action.
9. Moderation – Avoid extremes and judging others.
10. Keep clean in soul, body and spirit.
11. Tranquility – Do not sweat the little things and remorse over spilt milk. Clean it up and move forward.

12. Chastity – practice only for your health and offspring. Avoid publicity that would injure your own or another's reputation or peace of mind.
13. Humility – Ponder what Socrates or Jesus would do.

CONCLUSION

I wrote this for you, Brianna, when you were graduating from college with a B.A. in Communications. You are young and hopefully have a long boat ride down the River of Life. Keep this book and reread at Christmas and on your birthday. Review your successes and failures and write down your new plan.

Take notes and add them to this book so someday, you can distill new data and write your own story for your children.

The more things change, the more things stay the same. But regardless of what happens:

DO NOT GIVE UP!

I will be waiting for you when you reach the Gulf at the end of your ride on the River of Life. Take notes and add them to the book so you can write your story for your children.

PART II

The Way to Life, Liberty and The Pursuit of Happiness

Call L. Bruckner for coaching and questions, 815-259-3168
or bruck175@hotmail.com

ALL QUOTES ARE FROM THE AUTHORIZED KING JAMES
VERSION OF THE BIBLE PUBLISHED BY THE WORLD
SYNDICATE PUBLISHING COMPANY, CLEVELAND, OHIO.

GENESIS

In the beginning of the Bible Genesis is divided into three sections. The first one explains where man came from. It has the story of Adam and Eve and develops the concept of "SIN". It deals with the deluge, Noah's Ark. It provides a genealogy of patriarchs, explains the confusion of languages. It describes the symbol of SIN, the Tower of Babel. The second section establishes Jews as the chosen people of God with the call to Abraham. It highlights the struggles of brothers Esau and Jacob. The third section tells of Joseph's sale into slavery, his elevation in Pharaoh's government and the migration of his brother Jacob's family to Egypt.

We do not know what happens or why. Since the 1700's, man realized that fossils were the same found all over the world and that life evolved over millions of years. Species mutated and adapted to a changing environment (Darwin's theory) and perished. Did man come from aliens? Did interplanetary "angels" (robots) genetically transform apes into humans? Why are there different races? Who really built the pyramids??? Why are there boats buried underneath? Each discovery created more questions. The bottom line is we do not know what we do not know.

The two schools divided society. On one side is the religious demanding faith in the commands of an all powerful master – God. On the other side is science. They believe it's a hoax using mystery, miracles (rising from the dead) to scare and control. The problem with science is that there is no standard, no structure. What is right, what is wrong? Science is based on inductive reasoning. It starts with a presumed premise. If the premise is wrong, you get a false result or worse, a "cure worse than the disease". Example: indoor plumbing improved sanitation but the use of lead pipes caused lead poisoning.

In conclusion, you should retain standards while experimenting and exploring new ideas, methods and systems.

When you change how you See the World, it changes how you Think…
Which, in turn, changes how you Act… and how you React.
Which enhances your Relationships…and your Results.
Which farther opens up your horizons and changes your Whole World.

Enlightenment: Forget the Information Age. Enter the Age of Wisdom. Learn how to learn. See how to see. Think how to think.

EXODUS

Except for Genesis and the four Gospels of Jesus, this is probably the best story in the Bible. It describes the oppression of Jacob's descendants by Pharaoh. How Moses was adopted by Pharaoh's daughter and became a prince. It justifies why the tribes should be delivered by Moses, spend 40 years in the desert reforming society, enforce the law on Sinai (The 10 Commandments), breaking from worship of idols (the Golden Calf) and constructing a tabernacle. It forced worship of the One True God. It follows up on Genesis where the text briefly explains where humans came from, why Abraham and his descent were The Chosen People and got to Egypt.

Here in this book, we explore the 500 year cycle and the situation the world faces TODAY. The east led by China dominated the world from 1000 to 1500s. The Chinese between 1405 and 1433 under Zheng led seven (7) major expeditions with a fleet of 300 ships and 2800 sailors. (By comparison, Columbus's largest ship was only 85' long while the Chinese's largest ship was 400' long, 5x bigger!)

After exploring Africa, India and maybe America, the Chinese decided there was nothing "good" outside China so they burned the fleet, isolated the culture and defended themselves against the hordes from the north. Europe, on the other hand, used the Silk Road controlled by Muslims.

With the Eastern Roman Empire in Greece, Black Sea and Asia mines destroyed (Africa was cut off by Muslims); they turned to the sea. Spain, France, Portugal, England expanded south and west by the way of the sea and set off a 500-year cycle of growth, discovery (i.e. corn, potatoes, highest calorie content per acre with more energy, etc) that allowed Europe to exploit the world's resources. Now, Mao like Moses, sets out to transform society while expanding and controlling the trade routes.

Moses knew you cannot change a culture without destroying the old. In Egypt, the tribes were like zombies and slaves to a society that depended on Pharaoh. Today the U.S. is worse. A new study from the Congressional Budget Office concludes that 60% of all U.S. households now get more in transfer payments from the feds than they pay in taxes. The zombies vote. What do they vote for? Between 1988 and 2011, the percentage of the public that has been zombified by government transfer payments increases 62%. That leaves about 86 million full-time private-sector workers paying taxes...and 148 million on the receiving end. There are more than 100 million people in some kind of federal welfare program, 64 million on Social Security, 54 million on Medicare and 70 million on Medicaid. Since 2000, the rolls for food stamps increased by 17 million – bringing the total to 46 million. Today, the ratio of non-working people of working age to working people is almost 1:2. And the number of people on disability has soared. There were 51 working Americans to support every disabled person in 1968. Today, there are only 13. And those few stagger under the weight of so many zombies; they earn less than they did in the disco era.

People claim that increased productivity and AI will offset the rot in the work force but where is it coming from? Just 15 years ago, the traditional troika of the world's developed regions – the U.S., Japan and Europe – accounted for just over half of all industrial production. That means that half of the world's manufacturing (everything from iPhones to rocket engines), mining (gold, rare earth metals, and everything in between), and utilities (like electricity and gas) were generated in these areas. Emerging Asia, meanwhile – China, India, and nearly all the dozens of other countries in the region, from Vietnam to Sri Lanka – accounted for just 14 percent. About three-quarters of global industrial production growth came from emerging Asia. The region's share in total industrial production rose by nearly three times, to account for over one-third of the world's industrial output. Meanwhile, the combines share of the U.S., Europe and Japan fell to just 37 percent.

Add to that the fact of where people live.

This map can be summed up simply: a majority of the world's population live in Asia. That circle encompasses China, India, Indonesia, Bangladesh, Japan, Vietnam, the Philippines, Burma, Thailand, South Korea, Nepal, Malaysia, North Korea, Taiwan, Sri Lanka, Cambodia, Laos, Mongolia and Bhutan. More than 51% of the world's population live in those countries.

Mao, like Moses, cut the NOW from the past. Both instituted a "reform path of living". Moses prepared the people using Egyptian weapons and knowledge to seize the "Promised Land". China is investing $300 billion to finance a third of India's infrastructure projects over the next few years.

Part of that will modernize Indian railways as part of new economic opportunity corridors that stretch through India. China's five year plan builds a centralized, comprehensive development program. Using a low-cost labor force, they will build the belt "new railroad"(all the way to Rotterdam, Netherlands). The road will consist of a massive marine fleet to transport raw materials from Africa and South Asia. And China is doing the same thing in neighboring countries – Kazakhstan, Uzbekistan, Turkmenistan and Tajikistan. It is doing the same with Russia. The New Silk Road is a national strategy that draws on urbanizing the work force. Getting resources from wherever then they can steal them (it's intellectual property) controlling the food, energy and food supply.

Both movements will take two generations to mature. Exodus and Mao's "Red Book" both explain the roadmap they followed to lead their people into a "Promise Land".

SECRET: Duality: Forget rules. In nature, there are no rules. There's no one right way, no one best path. Everything is right and wrong, good and bad – often at the same time.

LEVITICUS, NUMBERS, DEUTERONOMY

In the Bible, these books state laws of sacrifices, feasts, and fasts, etc. Before stating the laws of life, let us explain why we believe in laws without coercion or pain. The masses almost never know the real reason for doing anything. The priest uses the following to enforce the law: <u>dogma</u>. The selected leaders declare their opinion as truth demanding people obey to stay in the flock. People crave the <u>approval</u> of other people in the herd so they repeat what is the fashionable opinion of the day. When <u>fashion</u> changes, so does their opinion. People's <u>egos</u> shape their acceptance of the laws. People adopt an image of themselves. For example, one aspires towards thinking of themselves as a "caring" person so they will select "caring" viewpoints. People also tend to adopt opinions in <u>empathy</u> with their heroes and role models or labels the family believes in.

People adore views expressed in simple, snappy slogan form. Because the herd wants safe and simple structures, the "elites" continue to control the narrative and few ask WHY or WHAT FOR. Before the outline of laws as in Leviticus, you should realize the cracks in American society that underlies all social problems. Unless it is stopped, the laws today will be sterile.

Fatherlessness destroys the social fabric of the family.

Cancerous tumors are killing the family. They are the perception that a father's primary contribution is only satisfying economic needs. Second: The sexual revolution of the 1960s perverted the philosophy that happiness of the INDIVIDUAL supersedes the welfare of the community. Finally, feminists weaken fatherhood while mass media replaced the strong image with the spineless father figure. All of these contribute to the negative trends of crime, poverty, educational failure, and teenage pregnancy, etc. Gone is the commitment to a child. As in Deuteronomy here are laws to live by:

- Eat a healthy breakfast; and do intermittent fasting (at least 12 hours between last and first meals)
- Move, walk, talk, drink water before and after exercising. Growing a garden provides movement, sunlight, microbes, organic fresh food and purpose. The weeds always need to be pulled.
- Protect joints and soft tissue by reducing animal foods. Eat foods that are alkaline to kill bacteria and viruses.
- Harness the power of your thoughts by adapting a Growth Mindset. Those who have a growth mindset see effort and learning as a way to grow. They understand that setbacks are a part of growth. Every day read, meet new people, strengthen your social network. Give 10% of your resources to others, NOT money but gifts, things, books, tapes, clothes, toys, pictures. Keep it light, happy and little but often. If you love to cook or bake, share your talents. We all like to eat something.

- Decide that you are a finisher, not in just one thing, but in all things. Decide what you want and why you want.

- Harness the incredible power of visualization. Think of the thing you would love to attain or achieve. Find a quiet place and let your body breathe. Immerse yourself in the achievement and take yourself through the steps perfectly visualizing how you feel. Visualize as if it were effortless and completely natural for you. I talk to myself every day and participate in a positive loving way.

- You must get more sunshine. If you raise a garden, you will get the sunshine from cultivating the plants and will get the benefit from high nutrient food that has not been contaminated with chemicals.

Always have purpose. Steer the boat <u>yourself</u> down the River of Life listening, watching, smelling ALL that Nature gives us.

Life is like the river, sometimes it sweeps you gently along and sometimes the rapids come out of nowhere.

"Wherever you go, you take yourself with you." --Neil Gaiman

Ignore the laws and SIN will be upon your soul.

JOSHUA

In the Bible, this book explains the progress from Moses to Joshua. It was a land grab; fighting to control the rich lands across the Jordan River. It outlines the return of the eastern tribes, the assignment of Levitical and refuge cities, the fall of Jericho and finally Joshua's farewell address pledging the people to fidelity.

Here we look at the five common denominators that led to Joshua's conquest of Palestine.

1. Choose the right skills that are in demand in today's society.
2. Create a habit of seeking financial independence rather than a display of social status.
3. Keep life simple by living beneath your means.
4. Allocate and prioritize time, energy and money more efficiently.
5. Be proficient in targeting opportunity you can act upon.

Do these goals sound almost too easy? Two simple problems have proven to stop 96.5% of the population from achieving these five goals! These two problems create an insidious lifestyle. When money looks good and people let the money burn a hole in their pocket, they are not ready for when financial resources fall. For every upward move, there are failures. Problems lead to stress, depression, bankruptcy, even death. No one has to be overwhelmed if they follow the legacy of our Founding Father, Thomas Jefferson.

In addition to his legacy as a Founding Father, Thomas Jefferson left us with his 10 Rules for a Good Life:

1. Never put off till tomorrow what you can do today.
2. Never trouble another for what you can do yourself.
3. Never spend your money before you have it.
4. Never buy what you do not want because it is cheap; it will never be dear to you
5. Pride costs us more than hunger, thirst, and cold.
6. Never repent of having eaten too little.
7. Nothing is troublesome that we do willingly.
8. Don't let the evils that have never happened cost you pain.
9. Always take things by their smooth handle.
10. When angry, count to 10 before you speak; if very angry, count to 100.

We are living in a high consumption environment. Even your family is being indoctrinated to SPEND, SPEND, SPEND. The solution is to save and defer immediate gratification. Jefferson's habits will provide self discipline. Relax and the desire will fade.

What resources did Joshua use to build society? Farmland is a very conservative hard asset. Ownership of farmland provides two important qualities we look for in an investment.

- First, it provides terrific asset appreciation potential. Indeed, the last few years have been an absolute boon for farmland investors. According to federal data, average prices for farmland rose by 50% between 2009 and 2013.
- Second, with continual production and sales to the markets, farms provide a steady stream of income.

Farmland is one of the best hedges against inflation, rising food prices, and societal uncertainty, as well as being the ultimate crisis hedge. Joshua wanted land. So do you.

After farmland, he wanted gold. WHY: Because like REAL ESTATE, it is REAL. Physical gold and silver have these advantages:

- To protect your wealth against currency devaluations. Since the inception of the Federal Reserve, the U.S. dollar has lost more than 98% of its value.
- To hedge against rising inflation and protect your purchasing power.
- To limit your exposure to another financial banking crisis.
- To reduce your exposure to foreign economic crises and geopolitical tensions.
- To limit your exposure to rising government debts, which threaten the safety and stability of the U.S. economy.

Third, Joshua did NOT have modern day REITs (**R**eal **E**state **I**nvestment **T**rust). Today you can invest in REITs.

Study, diversify. Beside REITs, look at Master Limited Partners where the company owns real property, i.e. pipelines, oil wells, storage units etc. Finally, have some real alternative investments you and your family enjoy, such as first edition books, jewelry, art, collectibles, guns, crossbows, and tools.

Joshua succeeded because he had a purpose for living. YOU must decide on the true pathway of living free and not an economic slave.

"For what shall it profit a man, if he shall gain the whole world, but lose his soul?" -Mark 8:36"

Ecology: Forget utopia. Nature doesn't recognize it. Every solution is merely the seed for more problems. Often, the new problem is an insidious version of the original problem.

Change is often desirable, frequently necessary, and always inevitable.

Ideas are funny things; they don't work until you do.

If you keep doing what you've always done, you'll always get what you've always gotten.

JUDGES, RUTH, SAMUEL I, II;
KINGS I, II, CHRONICLES

In the Bible, these book gives the history from the birth of Samuel, Saul, David, and Solomon followed by the building of the temple, and the deportation to Assyria-Babylon (after their defeat). Basically, it is the rise and fall of the country. It was a time of prosperity on the trade routes to and from the Black Sea to Egypt.

Here we will summarize what happened in the Golden years of prosperity in the U.S.A. from 1946 to 2001. In 1946, the U.S. had won the war. It was the only industrialized nation not destroyed by the fighting. The economy was driven by pent-up consumer demand. Consumer spending jumped from 56% of GDP to 65% in 1970 and 70% in 2000. Unionization and a wartime ethos created an environment where wage growth and employment within the races and classes was acceptable until 1970.

The baby boom exploded with new families needing housing, cars, food, clothing, etc. Children created excessive demand and people mortgaged their future to provide their needs. Expanded cultural consumption sparked a "Keeping Up With the Joneses" effort. When income inequality took off, the masses turned to excessive debt. Credit cards, second mortgages, student loans, etc became common.

Technology and globalization pushed expansion. Policies encouraged trade while muting nationalism. Movies, television, and computers provided a vision of worldwide growth, development and peace.

Scientific farming with fertilizers, hybrid seed, herbicides, and insecticides gave short term unsustainable food surpluses. More food, more babies. Vaccines (polio) and DDT drastically reduced the death rate. To keep the party going, the government worked to lower real interest rates. To expand globalization, "free trade" was demanded, tariffs dropped. The U.S.A. as the world reserve currency exploited cheap foreign labor to flood the country with Japanese goods and later China followed by Southern Asia.

The fabric of society was torn as the elites who had resources, knowledge and connections exploited the system creating massive compound wealth for the top 10% of the population.

To control the world society and support a growing defense/industrial complex, the government propped up dictatorships (sold arms) and engaged in numerous foreign wars. (Before 1961 who had ever heard of Viet Nam?)

When the elites realized the French and other foreign entities were draining the gold backing dollars at $35 per troy ounce (not at 1900 per ounce). Nixon simply "temporarily" suspended backing the dollar with gold. (Later Johnson debased the coinage taking away silver, even the little penny lost it's copper.)

To control the narrative, the government encouraged consolidation of the media. By 2016, Big Brother had the internet to finally make the printing press obsolete.

The tipping point came in 2007. Debt was consuming all growth, population birth rates had fallen (now we needed immigrants to spark demand.). The result was the economy collapsed and the federal reserve printed fake money to spin inflation. From 2007 to 2016, the qualitative easing worked. However, the masses realized that even with forcing the mother into the work force that the golden era was over. "Make America Great Again" won the day, but the creeping socialism continued with 62% of the population receiving some sort of government check whether it be Social Security, welfare, or they are working for the government. "Bread and Circus" anyone? The Federal Reserve in order to stabilize the economy, expanded monetary inflation by printing trillions of new dollars. Eventually the value of the dollar versus other currencies must fall. The elite who own or control tangible assets(land, gold etc) will increase their net worth at the expense of the laboring class.

SECRET: Resonance: Forget balance. It's illusion, and hence unattainable. Everything in nature is constantly resonating to and from the ideal, but always missing the mark.

EZRA, NEHEMIAH, ESTHER, JOB

Ezra deals with the first 42,000 Jews and their servants returning from captivity back to Palestine. Nehemiah continues where Ezra left off describing the rebuilding of the Temple, and reorganizing the government. Esther explained her denunciation of Haman's plot to exterminate the Jews. Her explanation justified permission for the Jews to defend themselves.

Job gives a face to the calamity caused by sin. When he submits to God's will, his prosperity returned.

In this book, we expose why we are trapped and then will be restored to prosperity. Unless the lessons of Nehemiah and Job are followed, we are unable to build an infrastructure supporting the American dream.

The problem is growth is significantly slower than the government is telling us. The historic productivity from 1870 to 1920 witnesses the internal combustion engine, paved roads, light bulbs, telephones, indoor plumbing, etc. From 1920 to 1970, new inventions like transistors, computers— leading to the world wide web—televisions, refrigeration, jet planes, atomic energy, etc., exploded the productivity rate. The bottom line is the industrial followed by the electronic revolution have squeezed the big gains of labor-saving devices. This leaves us a surplus of semi-skilled workers and a shortage of highly skilled technocrats to operate all the devices. We have concentrated the people into cities and streamlined supply-chains to a point of diminishing returns.

The Federal Reserve has become "god" using inflation as its remedy. It disguised a big tax upon savers, annuitants, and insurance policy holders. The trick worked until 2008 using paper currency to drastically increase the money supply. The money supply is dry tinder but it won't start the fire. Today's inflation is driven by demographics and behavioral psychology, two phenomena the Feds cannot control. In the U.S., the birth rate peaked in 1959 at 3.6 children per woman. By 2015, we were down to 1.9. Only illegal immigration keeps demand up. With debt growing and fewer babies coupled with a ballooning non-productive senior population, mobility stops and incites class warfare.

When people realize there is a lack of supply, or interest, or the debt increases the government deficit due to higher interest rates, then the growing debt will expand faster than inflation drives growth. Like Job, we need three friends. Like Nehemiah, stern measures are needed to be taken against greedy capitalists whoring the system. In the building of the defensive walls, Nehemiah had a plan of defense and laws to protect his people. Do we have walls to stop the flood of criminals crossing our borders????

What should you do NOW?

Individual investors may not be able to counter these head winds to global growth but they can prepare for further slowdowns and a possible liquidity crisis.

The first priority is to reduce allocations to the riskiest assets (stocks, corporate bonds, emerging markets) and increase allocations to liquid assets such as cash, Treasury notes and German government bonds. Acceptable currencies are U.S. dollars, euros and Swiss francs.

The second priority is to move some assets out of digital channels controlled by banks and brokers into physical channels controlled by you. This means buying physical assets, rental houses, and farmland. Control things you can use and enjoy!

*SECRET:*Stratification: Forget efficiency. Focus instead on effectiveness. Look to making every encounter completely worthwhile, every moment completely effective.

Aggregation: Forget independence. In nature, everything is interdependent, interconnected. But there's always a system to the chaos, a method to the madness. Look for these patterns. Network, network, network. We do not know what we do not know!

THE PSALMS ARE A SERIES OF POEMS, SAYINGS, AND WISE REFLECTIONS ON HUMAN BEHAVIOR

In the Bible, they are contributed to King Solomon because of the legend of his wise actions and policies. Probably the collection covers a wider period than his life. Probably many were set to music or recited like medieval chants. ALL were designed to bring peace of mind and remind the reader to worship God by setting a moral example of positive living during our short time on earth.

> For Yesterday is but a Dream,
> And Tomorrow is only a Vision;
> But Today well-lived makes every
> Yesterday a Dream of Happiness,

Before you speak, listen. Before you write, think. Before you spend, earn. Before you invest, investigate. Before you criticize, wait. Before you pray, forgive. Before you quit, try. Before you retire, save. Before you die, give. – William A Ward

Nothing in the world can take the place of persistence. Talent will not; nothing is more common than unsuccessful men with talent. Genius will not; unrewarded genius is almost a proverb. Education will not; the world is full of educated derelicts. Persistence and determination alone are omnipotent. --Calvin Coolidge

Don't live in the past thinking about mistakes or changes you made. Think of your life as a book, move forward, close one chapter and open another. Learn from your mistakes, but focus on your future, not on your past.

Slow Dance
Have you ever watched kids on a merry-go-round
Or listened to the rain slapping on the ground?

Ever followed a butterfly's erratic flight
Or gazed at the sun into the fading night?
You better slow down
Don't dance so fast
Time is short
The music won't last

You'd better slow down
Don't dance so fast
Time is short
The music won't last

Ever told your child, We'll do it tomorrow
And in your haste, not see his sorrow?

Ever lost touch, Let a good friendship die
'Cause you never had time to call and say "Hi"?

Life is not a race.
Do take it slower
Hear the music
Before the song is over.

Dust If You Must by Rose Milligan

Dust if you must, but bear in mind,
Old age will come and it's not kind.
And when you go (and go you must)
You, yourself, will make more dust.

Remember, a house becomes a home when
You can write "I love you" on the furniture.

PROVERBS

In the Bible, the Psalms (songs) and Proverbs were wise reflections on living. Not only were they learning tools but instruments to reduce anxieties, foster faith and courage, and overcome the trials of life. Below are a few modern reflections to ponder:

- Give God what's right – not what's left.
- Man's way leads to a hopeless end – God's way leads to an endless hope.
- A lot of kneeling will keep you in good standing.
- In the sentence of life, the devil may be a comma – but never let him be the period.

- When praying, don't give God instructions – just report for duty.
- Don't wait for six strong men to take you to church.
- We don't change God's message – His message changes us.
- When God ordains, He sustains.
- Plan ahead – It wasn't raining when Noah built the ark.
- Most people want to serve God, but only in an advisory position.
- Exercise daily – walk with the Lord.
- Nothing else ruins the truth like stretching it.
- Compassion is difficult to give away because it keeps coming back.
- He who angers you controls you.
- Give Satan an inch and he'll be a ruler.
- God doesn't call the qualified, He qualifies the called.
- Read the Bible – It will scare the hell out of you.
- In order to be free, you must reduce the external controls on your life.
- Be wary, many people seek to maximize their pleasures by conning your money, time, talent and energy.
- Very few people will choose the path of freedom and personal power.
- No person can become free until he unmasks the illusion of plagues, pride, lust, avarice, gluttony, usury, envy and sloth.
- The world is and always has been a very unfair place.
- Religions and cults are man-made inventions designed to allow the elitist "priesthood" to extract value out of those who follow them.

- Responsibility for what happens in Life rests solely with you.
- Successful relationships hinge upon a continued and approximate equal exchange of value between the parties.
- Why be normal? Seek greatness for the common good.
- Move out of your comfort zone and take calculated risks.
- Know that you have a purpose in living and in dying.
- Every pen holds a promise.
- Learn from your mistakes.
- Tourists see, but travelers seek adventures and insight. WHY?
- Asking for permission is asking for denial.
- Make friends who make you better.
- Big dreams start with small, unreasonable acts.
- Practice humility over hubris.
- Speak the language of the person you want to become.
- Have a purpose in what you do and say.
- Happiness is found in celebrating others' joys.
- There is only one chance at a first impression.
- Focus on one person in every room.
- Read the signs and listen to the sounds of the River of Life.
- Admit when you are wrong and ask forgiveness.
- Never take no from someone who can't say yes.
- Stick by your values, not your necessities.

The American Businessman

The American businessman was at the pier of a small coastal Panamanian village. One fisherman sat there with his small boat with 20 fish on the floor. The American asked how long it took to catch them.

The fisherman replied only a little while.

If it only took two hours, why didn't he stay out longer and catch more?

He replied he had enough to support his family.

The American then asked but what do you do with the rest of your time?

The fisherman said, "I sleep late, play with my children, go into the village each evening where I play the guitar with my friends."

The American thought for a minute and said, "I could help you. You should spend more time fishing and buy a bigger boat. With a bigger boat you could buy several boats, eventually you would have a fleet. By becoming big, you could cut out the middleman and sell directly to the processor, eventually opening your own cannery. By using vertical integration, you could have a lot of money and prestige. Eventually you could come to America."

The fisherman asked, "How long will this all take?"

The American replied, "15 years. Then you could retire."

He then asked, "What will I do when I retire?"

The American thought a long time. "You could sleep late, play with the family, and play your guitar while drinking beer with your friends."

He smiled. "I already have that NOW! Why stress out, grow old and come back in 15 years?"

He who only plans is a dreamer; he who only works is a drudge; but he who plans and works his plan is a conqueror.

It is common to overlook what is near by keeping the eye fixed on something remote. –Samuel Johnson

We ourselves feel that what we are doing is just a drop in the ocean. But the ocean would be less because of that missing drop. -- Mother Teresa

You will never find time for anything. If you want time, you must take it. – Charles Buxton

Yesterday is a cancelled check.
Tomorrow is a promissory note.
Today is the only cash you have – spend it wisely.

It is easier to resist at the beginning of things than at the end. – Seneca

Since we cannot change reality, let us change the eyes which see reality. – Nikos Kazantzakis

Listen to the whispers and you won't have to hear the screams. – Cherokee Saying

Do not go where the path may lead, go instead where there is no path and leave a trail. – Ralph Waldo Emerson

Forgiving those who hurt us is the key to personal peace. – G. Weatherly

ECCLESIASTES

This book in the Bible deals with happiness, accumulation of wealth, appropriate seasons for everything, and the incomprehensible anomalies in life. While projecting a poetic picture of old age, the conclusion is to fear God and keep his commandments.

Here we example fears and fate like death we have no control over.

Fear 1. Kings and Prime Ministers or presidents do NOT control their economies. If they could, we would never have recessions (look at corona virus).

Political leaders and the elite can prevent inflation with fiscal and monetary management BUT THEY CANNOT PREVENT ECONOMIC DOWNTURNS. WHY??? Weather controls the environment. Volcanic activity, solar cycles and the earth's magnetic field are to be feared. Beside the peace dividend after WWII, we have lived through 60 years of the best weather in the last 1200 years. Sulfuric acid from volcanoes is incredible. In 1816, there was snow each month of the year in the northern hemisphere. Boston had 14" of snow on June 29. While many worry about carbon from coal warming the planet, we could be into a cycle of cold and dry conditions. Dryness leads to drought, drought leads to starvation. Hungry people move and wars for resources explode.

Fear II. What cycles are we in NOW? Here are six different cycles that all will hit in October 2020. This hasn't happened since 1929.

1. The Kondratieff cycle is shortening now from about 55 years to about 30 years due to debt. This is a subject for future studies. Peak was Real Estate Bust in 2007.
2. The Juglar cycle. This one is part of the yearly cycle for stocks. It should bottom in 2027 after its bottom in early 2008.
3. Kuznet Cycle—This 18-year cycle shows the real high in income inequality. The real high isn't due until 2024-2025.
4. Kitchin Cycle—Named after Jim Kitchin who tied this with the real estate cycle. The bottom won't be until 2020-2022.
5. The 20- and 60-Year Macro Economic Cycles. This is one of the really dominant cycles which follow interest rates. Interest rates should peak about 2020-2022 and also about 2045—which are tied to the war cycles between 2012 and 2020 and also 2036-2042.
6. Commodity Depression Cycle. There are really two of them, but the main one is 30 years in length. It last bottomed in the mid-1980s and had its next bottom in February 2020.

The bad thing is most of the cycles are on the down side.

Even though you cannot change the spiral nor the direction, you must be able to integrate the cycle into your life. Your senses, feelings and judgment are aroused in the following order. First, you are curious (why is this happening? How does it bring pain, change and disruption?) When it really sinks in, you have a sense of loss or fear of loss. You are scared, hoard things, and lose courage to adventure or ACT. Once you understand the situation, fear turns to greed and you gain a sense of gain. Once you gain the confidence of gain, you become afraid of being left behind. Urgency governs your actions. Finally the fifth phase is a sense of reliability. Habits, traditions are formed; steady low decline sets in until the next cycle begins with curiosity of something NEW.

As you respond to the circle of life, there are two important factors to adjust in your life. Study the Consumer Life Spending Cycle.

Figure 1-1: Consumer Life Cycle

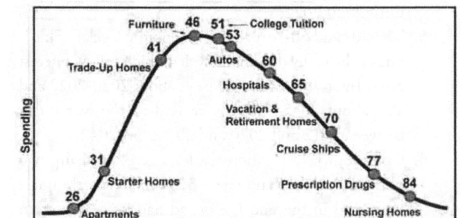

Data Source: U.S. Census Bureau, Dent Research

The actual peak is at age 46 for the average household and 54 for the most affluent. Between ages 46 and 64 our spending habits tend to change dramatically. We see retirement not far off and make a concerted effort to save, while our spending needs decline as our kids leave the nest. We retire at age 63 (on average) and tend to have our greatest net worth at age 64 – cash, investments, and assets we've set aside to live on.

Know where you fit in.

Lastly, research shows we function of a 23-day physical cycle, 28-day emotional cycle and a 33-day intellectual curve. Study your OWN life, plot how you feel, react and live. You may have to adjust the duration for yourself. Remember you are stronger, more relaxed and smarter on the first ½ of the cycle, weaker on the downside. Since the cycles have different durations, you need to plot three separate trials. At one time, all can be up or down—beware and act accordingly. Remember the cycles are a spiral swing down the River of Life.

Paralyze resistance with persistence.

Our greatest glory is not in never failing, but in rising every time we fall. – Confucius

Consider how hard it is to change yourself and you will understand how hard it is to change others.

JEREMIAH, LAMENTATIONS, ISAIAH

These books deal with the fall of Jerusalem and the captivation of Baghdad. The books deal with temptation, evil ways, and the lack of discipline in keeping the faith to God. Read the book for the prophet's view on how and why to maintain the Jewish tribal identity in a strange, hostile world.

This chapter is simply a checklist of items you need if you are forced from your home to either a safe house or leaving because of a political change (military coup) or a climate or natural disaster (meteorite, earthquake, etc) or starvation.

The first thing you will want to have is a tactical flashlight.

The second item is a battery-powered or hand-cranked radio that includes the NOAA weather station.

The third item is a hand-cranked charger needed to recharge the batteries for the flashlight, the radio and any other small rechargeable power tools or medical equipment.

But I say unto you, Love your enemies, bless them that curse you, do good to them that hate you, and pray for them which despitefully use you… Matthew 5:44

OTHER ITEMS YOU MIGHT WANT TO CONSIDER

Emergency money: cash, gold and silver coins (paper may be worthless)

A first aid kit and any special medications and/or foods needed by infants or elderly

One complete change of clothing and footwear per person

Sturdy shoes or work boots

Raingear

Blankets and sleeping bags

Warm hats and gloves (location dependent)

Enough tents to house all family members

Games and books: don't depend on computers; take laptop and mobile phone but don't depend on them.

Extra reading and prescription glasses

Sunglasses and sun block

Emergency-preparedness manual; cookbook

Utility knife

Comprehensive tool kit with hammer and nails

Duct tape (several rolls)

Matches in a waterproof container

Compass (optional)

Water and collapsible plastic containers for extra water and wine

Aluminum foil

Paper towels

Paper and pencil

Needle and thread

Whistle; guns, ammunition

EZEKIEL 26, DANIEL 28

In the Bible, the book of Ezekiel deals with the destruction of Jerusalem. Both deal with crises of how to survive. Both demand faith in God. Beyond that, you need knowledge. You need a written crises/survival plan. Do a drill every six (6) months with ALL the family. Have your youngest children who read and comprehend, exercise the drill. Each plan varies based on location, resources and nature of crises. Fire, accidents (car), wind and water (hurricanes cause the most incidents). It is one thing to conduct a drill and another when stressed, panicked and blood is squirting everywhere. Here we summarize what you need to survive a crisis.

First you need to have food. If you've ever been in the military, then you're probably familiar with an MRE, otherwise known as a "Meal, Ready-to-Eat." They're self-contained, lightweight field rations given to military personnel for use in combat or when there aren't formal food facilities.

Then turn to a survival blueprint. Here is a list of items you start stockpiling today to protect yourself from whatever problems may come down the road:

1. Distilled or canned water – It's not food, but it's essential to life. Let's face it: Having guns and a shelter to keep you safe is nice. But it means nothing if you and your family are dying of thirst after a few days. If

necessary, treat the water with chlorine bleach. Let it sit for 60 minutes before drinking.

2. Oats and oatmeal – It's low in saturated fat and also a good source of protein. If it was good enough for American pioneers, then it's good enough for you.

3. Powdered milk – Some brands can last up to two years.

4. Protein bars and protein drinks – Whey contains the essential amino acids that your body needs. Combine with milk to maximize nutritional value.

5. Corn – It's a pantry essential.

6. Oils – Oil is an essential cooking ingredient. Stock up on olive and coconut oil, ghee, butter, and lard.

7. Coffee, tea and meat-stock cubes (they add flavor to any meal).

8. Hard cheese encased in wax – The wax prevents cheese from growing mold and keeps the moisture in. It can also be stored without refrigeration.

9. Canned liquids – Pineapple and vegetable juice

10. Sugars and molasses – Granulated, brown, and powdered sugar are the way to go.

11. Iodized salt – It's more than just a food seasoning. Salt helps regulate fluids in the body, kills bacteria, and can help you avoid problems with your thyroid gland.

12. Honey – Even if you don't plan on using it, buy honey anyway. The stuff never goes bad.

13. Nuts, seeds and nut butters – Nuts can go rancid very quickly, but they're an excellent source of vital nutrients.

14. Beans and legumes – A pound of beans contains 1,250 calories. Keep them dry and they will last.

15. Canned vegetables and fruits

16. Raisins, dried fruits and fruit strips – A handful of raisins could provide you with the name nutritional value as a full serving of fruit.

17. Pastas – Dried pastas have little or no moisture so they will last.

18. Rice – Jasmine rice is cheap and easy to store.

19. Crackers – They have little nutritional value but are filling.

20. Food Bars – Compact nutrition that's easy to store and even easier to carry.

21. Vodka, whiskey and smokes – You're going to want a substance that can be used for cooking, or clean cuts and wounds or barter for other goods.

22. Baking soda and baking powder – The former can be used with other ingredients like buttermilk and yogurt to make baked goods rise.

23. Can opener and a pot for cooking, etc.

After food, water and shelter, these are items you need in your survival bags.

A. Clothes. If things get really bad, you'll soon realize the clothes you have on will go only so far. Consider packing the clothes you would wear if you were going backpacking/hiking/camping for a weekend: a sturdy pair of boots, long pants, two pairs of socks, shirts, and a jacket that will keep you warm, thermal underwear, a hat, and a bandana.

B. Basic gear. Don't forget the essentials. These include waterproof matches, rain gear, a flashlight with spare batteries, cooking tools, and a sharp knife or two. Remember, your matches will eventually run out, so consider learning how to use a fire-starting kit.

C. Weapons. If things get bad, the world will get dangerous. That's why one of the most important things you can have in your bag is a tool to keep you and your family safe. A gun is probably your best; don't forget ammunition.

D. First-aid kit. Spend enough time outside your comfort zone and you're bound to get hurt so have a kit and KNOW HOW TO USE IT.

E. Finally, have candles, batteries, radio, watch, toilet paper and sleeping bags.

Remember, negative panic is an evolutionary involuntary coping mechanism that feigns DEATH. It strikes people who are terrified and trapped. Playing dead might cause the saber-toothed tiger to not eat you but in a fire, negative panic leads to death. To avoid negative panic, recognize the three (3) states in a crisis.

- ■ Disbelief: it's not really happening
- ■ Deliberation: people try to figure out what is happening
- ■ Decisiveness: action

You want to get passed 1 and 2 quickly and ACT rationally. Faith that God will help you prevail is essential. Faith gives you the shield and discipline to confront the lions. Realistic optimism, preparation and practice will end the trapped response, heal helplessness, overcome isolation (God is always with thee) and calm the impulse to overreact (jumping out the window).

After protecting, you are NOT too hot or cold so you think rationally and remember the Rule of 3 as it helps you keep your survival priorities in order. The Rule of 3 states you cannot survive:

3 seconds without spirit and hope
3 minutes without air
3 hours without shelter in extreme conditions
3 days without water
3 weeks without food
3 months without companionship or love.

In the Bible, it deals with commitment. Here we briefly look at why we are committed to a system. Loss of commitment is destroying society. It deals with the approaching judgment. Daniel gives us his deliverance from the lion's den, his vision of four angels, and revelation of the time of the END.

The great mass of people almost never know their real reason for doing anything. In this sense, they blindly stumble along, in any old direction, allowing themselves to be pushed and pulled by almost any external force. Their 'response' has no basis in logic, it is simply a knee-jerk reaction founded in prejudice, habit, or any one of the following erroneous reasons:

1. Dogma. This is defined as an 'arrogant declaration of opinion, especially associated with the church'.
2. Empathy. We aspire to be like our heroes.
3. Ego. People hold views and opinions on issues because the image they have of themselves demands that they hold certain views. If they aspire towards thinking of themselves as a 'caring' person, then they will trot-out a selection of 'caring' viewpoints.
4. Fashion. People repeat fashionable opinions because they are insecure and they need the approval of other people. They will instantly change their opinions as soon as fashion dictates.
5. Labels. This involves holding opinions because those opinions agree with previously set-up labels. If for example, you labeled gypsies as "rogues 'n' thieves", then they adopt a position supporting the label.
6. Safe and Simple. This is perhaps the most common reason for holding erroneous opinions. People are lazy and stupid. People instantly decide who is the 'good guy' and who the 'bad guy' is, and they become upset, confused and angry if there are any grey areas. Mass media has reinforced this laziness.
7. Vested Interest. This is simply holding an opinion because you have a vested interest in the outcome and not because you believe it to be true.
8. Association. People scramble over one another to adopt an opinion on an issue because of the association the issue has, with other, unrelated issues. If the herd feels something is bad, then most people go with the herd.

Secret: "The search for ultimate truth is erroneous. There is no such thing. Conventional popular morality is merely a function of your latitude and longitude and the date currently on the calendar."

Humans have invented moral codes with a view to surviving without pain and suffering. We place restrictions on ourselves voluntarily for the 'greater good'. Vast amounts of propaganda, rules and regulations are required to convince everyone that it is in their 'own interests' to STAY DOCILE. They want a society designed to keep everyone firmly in their place. Remember it is easier to steal from others then work to hunt or grow your own food.

Religion and morals are invented by us.

Moral codes are invented by man to allow us to live together with minimum pain, it is trivially obvious that these morals should (and do) change with circumstances. Throughout history, morals have shifted and changed according to fashion and circumstance as described early why people believe. Science has a difficult time changing culture.

In conclusion, morality depends upon your level of enlightenment. It might not be considered 'immoral' for a Lion to rip your head off, but highly immoral for another man to do so. It depends on where you are 'coming from'. For example, moral dilemmas involve balancing different actions in order to determine which is 'worse'. Is it 'worse' to shoot someone through the head, or stand and watch that same man drowning without throwing him the life belt you have in hand? Which is 'better: to not talk a man out of suicide and watch him kill himself, or to administer poison to him if he begs you to end his life for him? Religion, especially

Christianity, tries to shroud everything in "LOVE" in order to first get you to avoid moral crises. If that fails, it provides salvation and forgiveness to reduce guilt and anxiety over your failure to solve the problems.

Like the prophets society failing because of
vanishing fatherhood. Government's "Big Brother"
is working to make "group think" and not the
family as the building block for living.

OBADIAH, JONAH, MICAH, NABIUM, HABAKKUK, ZEPHANIAH, HAGGAI, ZECHARIAH, MALACHI

All of these books survived because they deal with the corruption of the nation, unhealthy sin in society, the Day of Judgment for people's actions, neglect of the Temple and its teachers, the apocalyptic vision and the coming of a Messiah to set matters straight. All of these books, arranged at the end of the "Old Testament", set up the New Testament with four different versions of Jesus' life and teachings.

Whether you are waiting for the Messiah or as a Christian preparing for the second coming of Christ, here are 12 principles to keep your life on a healthy tract. Preparing today for the "Judgment Day":

1. The mind is the single most powerful thing in the universe.
2. Positive Mental Attitude draws you to things: people and circumstances that help you achieve your objectives.
3. Eliminate all draining people to achieve great success.
4. Self-discipline is acting intellectually and prudently, not for instant gratification.
5. Go placidly amidst the noise and haste; remember what peace there may be in silence.
6. To focus you must live, sleep, and breathe your focus.
7. There's an offsetting positive to every negative situation you encounter.
8. There is direct correlation between reality and that which the mind visualizes.
9. Mystery commands respect.
10. All unhappiness is caused by attachment. Enjoy life and what you achieve, but don't become attached to it.
11. Exercise caution in your business affairs; for the world is full of trickery.
12. With all its sham, drudgery, and broken dreams, it is still a beautiful world. Be careful. Strive to be happy.

THE GOSPELS

There are four (4) books written down 200 years after Jesus' death to describe his life and teachings. Each one was selected to convert different audiences. When Constantine, who was considered a living God, was baptized on his deathbed, it led to the conversion of the entire Roman Empire. What is the core of Christian belief?

Matthew 5:6-7 New International Version:

Verse 6: Blessed are those who hunger and thirst for righteousness, for they will be filled.

Verse 7: Blessed are the merciful, for they will be shown mercy. Because there was no written text, many changes were made. It was not codified until the Council of Nicene. Many gospels were omitted. We will never know the real story. Even after the Greek translated was produce for example, the story of the virgin birth and the seven sacraments were added by the Pope.

It is imperative that you read the parables in the four different gospel versions that were written and produced at different times for different audiences and reasons. Especially take time to read the "Sermon on the Mount" which summarizes the teachings of Jesus. The result was that the new Christian religion taught through baptism and faith in Jesus Christ that the world should treat the poor, the disadvantages, the orphaned, the widow with equal status with those of privilege and wealth. Secondly through forgiveness and faith, the followers believed in forgiveness of sins and redemption of the soul. Finally, the new religion gave comfort to answering the question of all religious doctrines of where we are and where we are going. The Christians with the belief of the holy trinity, proclaimed that physical death was just a phase in your existence and that your soul went to a better place where there is no suffering and pain.

ACTS

In the Bible, this comes right after the four gospels (different versions of Jesus preaching for different audiences and times). Acts describes the descent of the Holy Spirit and adopts the principle of 3 (Trinity). It describes the ascension of Jesus to a God-like status, due to apostolic miracles. It gives concrete structure to the Christian decline by outlining the arrest, defense and execution of Stephen. It summarizes Peter's vision of a Church and finally glorifies the conversion of Saul of Tarsus AKA Paul and his three missionary journeys and ending in his trials, using his Roman citizenship in Rome.

In this paragraph, we summarize ACTS you need to do NOW.

If you remember only one thing from these three sections,

all religions and organized society, whether in the family or the American empire, try to cancel the concept THAT VIOLENCE PAYS. It is the easiest way to get something, just take it. It came into practice when the first caveman realized he could sharpen a stone tool and beat his neighbor across his Neanderthal skull with it. No longer did he have to spend all day hunting and gathering.

He could accumulate three times as much as he did the day before with very little energy and in the fraction of the time. Saving his energy to trap women, enjoy his pleasure and produce babies. (Poor women, they had all the pain of birth and the struggle to feed the little bastards.)

The cost and benefits of using violence determines the way societies organize. Power has always sought the easiest road to wealth by attacking those who have it. Wars change the rules. Because violence pays so well, it is hard to control. Gunpowder, the stirrup, and the cross bow are all rooted in violence. Insights into violence offer a framework of how society will be reconfigured. As an example, will the U.S.A. succeed in taking back the resources needed to continue growing all the while maintaining the dollar as the world's reserve currency or will the Chinese out flank us through the UN or a third world war???

Now you know violence is the bedrock of society and appreciate why organized society and religion must control this fact. What ACTS should YOU DO?!!

I can't-Will literally stop growth
I won't -Will literally put a block in your way
It's hard- is a command to self

I Don't Believe-Will literally stop you from achieving anything in your life

I'm a skeptic-Is a taught behavior that is a conditional to hold a person back

I don't like it-Stops a person from learning/Stops a person from gaining intellect (IQ)

Now with a proper mindset, you need an ACTION foundation.

Honesty is the only way to make money in today's world. But here's the truth. Dishonesty works…until it doesn't.

Everyone makes mistakes. When you are dishonest, you are given only one chance and then it's over. You're out of the game.

When you are honest, people will trust your word and spread the news that you are a person to be sought out, sought after, given opportunity, given help, or given money.

Here are methods to display your genuine honest <u>work</u> ethic and ACTION.

1. Do what you say you are going to do.
2. Enhance the lives of others.
3. Don't lead a double life. It saps energy. Someone will expose your fraud and you will lose all your gains.
4. Take the blame. If you mess up opening, be man or woman enough and try to make it right.
5. Give credit to others even if it is your sole idea. It builds trust and networks.
6. Be the source. People will turn to you for more ideas. Have a positive vision.

7. Don't be angry. It is a form of dishonesty. It is a lie to expect people around you to be perfect. DO NOT BLAME OTHERS.
8. No excuses. Use it as a learning exercise. Do not use a cover-up to hide failure. Do not give up.
9. Don't gossip. Even if it is true, you lose the opportunity to build trust and relationships.
10. Make others look good. This ties back into giving credit to others. Make people feel special.
11. Introduce two people. If you want to grow, you need help. If they grow and prosper, so will you.

When you are honest, you will have nobody to run from. Some people will hate you. Some people will doubt your sincerity. But the people who need someone to call, someone to share with, or someone to give to, these people will know who to call. They will call and trust you.

Now that you have a grand plan, where do you start?

Your personal Master Plan will not only be the foundation but also the blueprint of your success.

    a. Write down your Life's Goals.
    b. Make a list of everything you want to do (some call this a bucket list).
    c. Narrow down to ten (10) choices.
    d. Narrow down to four (4) goals.
    e. Pick one goal to start today.
    f. Make a 5-year and a 1-year roadmap.

The secret to success is not attitude but action. Shallow people believe in luck. Strong people believe in cause and effect. Promise yourself at the end of each meeting or day, you will either have improved someone's impression of you or secured for yourself some business advantage. Always look into the eyes and repeat before sleep the above actions.

Once you are on your honest road to happiness, here are a few tricks to make the trip easier.

- No impulse buying; use 24-hour rule before buying anything over $100; analyze what is it really worth
- get a checking account with no bank fee
- cut cable costs; go to ROKU or other streaming services
- use library (it's free) or other free download source such as Project Gutenberg
- work out at home; get programs on TV or from your library (no need for expensive gym memberships)
- stop smoking; reduce drinking to social settings
- make your coffee at home; reduce visits to Starbucks
- copy your keys
- clean out your house; patch and repair
- purchase store brands unless you have coupons for name brands or it's on sale
- don't buy lottery tickets (waste of money)
- no storage units; keep only what you need and use
- stop trying to keep up with the Jones's
- know your limits
- check out housing options
- some items can be purchased used (EBay, Craig's List, tag sales, etc)

"It is the mark of an educated mind to be able to entertain a thought without accepting it." --Aristotle

"Science is organized knowledge. Wisdom is organized life." --Immanuel Kant

"Happiness is a Gift and the trick is not to expect it but to delight in it when it comes. And to add to other people's store of it." --Charles Dickens

"Humor can get in under the door while seriousness is still fumbling at the handle." --G.K. Chesterton

"Knowledge speaks, but wisdom listens." --Jimi Hendrix

CORINTHIANS I AND II, GALATIANS

In the Bible, these books deal with the decision-making struggle of new Christians that were of Jewish heritage. People had a real problem balancing the Jewish traditions with the coming resurrection of Christ, while teaching followers who obeyed Jewish rites and ceremonies. New followers had mental roadblocks in making difficult decisions following Paul's teachings. Simply, there are no laws that supersede the glory of the cross and a pathway walking/living in the spirit.

This book provides measures to handle mental roadblocks and makes it easier to decide on a course of action.

There are three common mental roadblocks.

ROADBLOCK #1: <u>Wishful Thinking</u>

Wishing is passive. We wish for things over which we have little or no control. Wishes have the language full of regrets about past decisions. We wish we'd taken the other job. We wish we hadn't let the love of our life get away. On the other hand, dreaming is different. Dreams are active. We can actually do something about a dream. Dreams are a form of real vision initiation. You dream of getting something or someone. You dream of dropping Jewish lore and following a new path of removing sin by practicing love, mercy and grace toward everyone, not just your Jewish tribe.

ROADBLOCK #2: <u>What If Everyone Thinks You're Crazy?</u>

Family approval does matter. Change is painful. When the people we love fail to support or actually take away family, friends and resources you need to make change, it <u>hurts</u>.

ROADBLOCK #3: <u>Fear of Change</u>

Try to reason with the core family to change with you. Here are six weapons to help in your transformation. Good decision-making requires intelligence, experience, and judgment.

A. Figure out what you want. Write down the benefits that will come to you and your loved ones. Explain what is most important and what you can live without.

B. Consider the expense of indecision. If you can't make up your mind and do nothing, what will it cost you?

C. Set a deadline for making a decision or just decide not to make one at all. Nothing is worse than dragging out the process. Simply end it.

D. Consider the pros and cons, the risks and rewards. Figure out the worst possible outcome of any contemplated decision. Why are you considering the changes? Is it <u>really</u> important? Will you go to HELL if you are not SAVED by the blood on the cross???

E. Ask the advice of other sinners who have had to make similar decisions.

F. Remember point C.

Once you make a decision, i.e. to change jobs, put extra effort into studying how the new job actually WORKS and how you can help others improve the <u>daily outcome</u>.

I always have option A, option B and then a disaster plan C. Give it your best effort and FORGIVE THOSE WHO TRY TO STOP YOU.

"Which of you, by being anxious, can add one moment to his lifespan?" Matthew 6:27

Regrets steal joy from the past, anxiety steals opportunity from the future. Both steal energy from the present. Anxiety is the opposite of self care.

EPHESIANS

It's a book of benediction, sort of a Thanksgiving to God for the grace proceeding from the atonement. The emphasis is on a common bond between Jesus and Gentiles. It explores ways leading to unity notwithstanding the diversity of talents. It shows why diversity is necessary because different duties, cultures, sex (male vs. female) are needed to walk in the spirit. Sin is renounced and a simple understanding of how Christ and the Church are a union.

In this book, outlines 21 ways to strengthen the unions of labor and capital to produce the best product or service.

1. The business meets a demand and consistent need.
2. Company has a very good knowledge of the competition and their practice (is this a nook).
3. Company is not dependent on one source of supply or one's customers (client).
4. Suppliers and vendors are true partners (tie them in to shares/profits).
5. Vision, mission, goals and stratagems are understood by all associates (workers).
6. Procedures to measure client satisfaction and why others do not buy your service.

7. Quarterly schedule source of money meetings, review of market strengths, weaknesses, efficiencies, goals — all support the program.

8. Is there adequate resources and cash flow to support business plan for at least six (6) months?

9. Are team associates held accountable? No excuses for failure (lesson of experience).

10. Is approach positive, enjoyable, quality, pride, rated by importance, systems?

11. Constant review for synergy, positive change, fully utilized associate's ability.

12. Reports and suggestions seriously considered with written analysis onr what do we lack?

13. Read, review study other management, leadership, business options.

14. Open up to delegate duties, encourage network, innovation, AI, computers.

15. Prioritize TIME — work no more than 50 weeks, take meaningful vacation.

16. Build healthy work climate, food, exercise, saving for ALL financially.

17. Deadlines are established and adhered to — excuses are examined and corrected.

18. Meetings have written agenda, specific objectives and outcome then ACTION.

19. Advertise only what we can test, measure the results.

20. Spend quality time with the people you care about. Time and health are MORE IMPORTANT THAN MONEY. MANAGE STRESS VERY CAREFULLY.

21. Don't forget to say "THANK YOU", remember the manager's birthdays, events, etc.

PHILIPPIANS AND COLOSSIANS

Paul is in prison and grateful to his friends in Philippi. He is indifferent to death because death brings him sooner to the presence of Christ. He looks at the world and warns of false teachers. He thinks you can find the way yourself!! You do not need distraction and costs that lead you to suffering and bad social environments.

This book explores other options to traditional college but rather the pathway to helping the greatest number of souls. As an alternative, consider studying at uncollege.com for free and see what really interests you:

- MIT Open Course Ware: Follow the curriculum guides to get a free MIT education. Various multimedia and resources for each course.
- The Open University: 600+ free online classes with exercises. Track progress. Use forum. Intro to advanced classes.
- UC Irvine OCW: 190 UC Irvine courses.
- Harvard Med School OCWI: 115+ Harvard Medical School courses.

- OCW Consortium: For more Open Course Ware universities, see current members, including 22 U.S. universities and many from around the world.

Many jobs do not need a four year diploma. Attend community college. In just two years' time, students can earn an associate degree or a certification as a veterinary technician, a dental hygienist, web designer or even a winemaker. Community college also affords you the option of transferring to a four-year college after receiving your associate degree. We need skills.

Don't forget travel. When you travel, you leave behind the familiar and take on a world of new things. You're constantly learning through travel, with new cultures, friends, foods and languages. Traveling has the ability to take you out of your daily routine and into new surroundings and experiences and this can reset your body and mind. ... This keeps the mind sharp, increases creativity and helps with personal growth.

Remember there are five (5) steps in life:

1. Death is Certain.
2. Innovation takes place NONSTOP
3. There is No teaching, only learning.
4. Keep learning.
5. GROW

There are growing trends that we need to examine:

Trend #1: Financial Technology: a cashless society using Bitcoin and Block Chain will destroy the U.S. dollar monopoly as the world reserve currency hurts U.S. citizens but helps everyone else.

Trend #2: Robotics: MIT professor Rodney Brooks said that robots don't have to start out "smart". They can figure out lots of small things along the way—just like humans. What do robots need? They are hungry for technology, for more powerful batteries. Every battery uses lithium (go into mining).

Trend #3: The temp workforce: Uber is the perfect example of one of these companies. It allows people who are out of work, but who have a nice car, to make some money with very little commitment or overhead.

Trend #4: The aging population: 73 million baby boomers need services. Companies need to rise up to address these various problems and needs.

Trend #5: Healthcare: Not only the old but everyone needs it. The idea that healthcare is a right will cause products and services to explode.

Trend #6: Surveillance: Big Brother is here to stay. The prison industry grows and security is everywhere.

Trend #7: Chemistry, Climate Change, CO_2, H_2, etc.: Chemistry is going to be much more influential in the coming years—more so even than information technology is now. Computers and information technology were big in the '70s, '80s, '90's but that trend is behind alternative energy, battery storage, new drugs and DNA processes.

John 8:7: "He that is without sin among you, let him first cast a stone at her."

Honesty is a muscle.

THESSALONIANS I AND II

These were written to praise growth, patience and prayer. Many followers wanted to know why the Second Coming has NOT come (We are still waiting 1900 years later). To deflect their depression, persecution and demand for action, the book gives excuses why the Lord is delayed. It couples the dead with the living by exhortation of purity and loving remembrance of the living and the dead.

In this book, we bring light to ways to live longer.

1. GET FIDGETY
2. BETTER YET, WALK
3. TAKE THE STAIRS—EVERY DAY
4. BEWARE THE HIGH-TECH DASH
5. MAKE PEACE WITH FAMILY AND REDUCE STRESS.
6. MONITOR YOURSELF
7. TRY TO STAY OUT OF THE HOSPITAL. GET SOCIAL
8. GET A FRIEND WITH FOUR LEGS
9. VACATION…OR ELSE
10. SAVE YOUR PENNIES

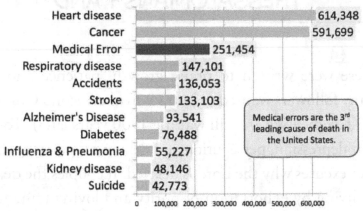

Medical Error The 3rd Leading Cause of Death

Cause	Deaths
Heart disease	614,348
Cancer	591,699
Medical Error	251,454
Respiratory disease	147,101
Accidents	136,053
Stroke	133,103
Alzheimer's Disease	93,541
Diabetes	76,488
Influenza & Pneumonia	55,227
Kidney disease	48,146
Suicide	42,773

Medical errors are the 3rd leading cause of death in the United States.

0   100,000 200,000 300,000 400,000 500,000 600,000

Sources: CDC. National Center for Health Statistics. Number of deaths for leading causes of death, 2014.

11.
12. EAT LESS
13. JUST ADD WATER
14. DON'T SWEETEN WITH SUGAR
15. COFFEE
16. RIPENESS MATTERS
17. MARRIAGE
18. PLEASE GO TO BED
19. CUT BACK ON PAIN PILLS
20. GET OUT AND EXERCISE TO GET VITAMIN D FROM SUNLIGHT
21. DRINK WHOLE ORGANIC MILK
22. EAT WHOLE GRAINS
23. EAT YOUR VEGGIES
24. DRINK LESS ALCOHOL
25. GO NUTS
26. CONSIDER MOUNTAIN LIFE

Matthew 7:14: Because narrow is the gate and difficult is the way which leads to life, and there are few who find it.

Nothing that is difficult for you is fun. If it were easy, everyone would do it.

Key: The person who can learn from everything will beat out the person who judges harshly who and what to learn from. Sometimes skeptics fool themselves. They replace god with self-help gurus. They replace mystery with unproven science. "I believe only if I can see." Science is open mindedness, questions, curiosity and learning.

It is not the strongest or the most intelligent who will survive but those who can best manage change.

TIMOTHY, TITUS AND PHILEMON

These books deals with the kind of men who should be ordained as bishops and elders. They contain instruction of how to confront the events in Crete, and avoid unprofitable situations. They have a stern warning to be wary of heretics that divert people away from the true way.

The book explains how to train leaders.

- People learn better when they're actively involved in the learning process.
- People learn better when they're using as many senses as possible.
- People retain about:
  - 10% of what they hear
  - 30% of what they read
  - 50% of what they see
  - 90% of what they do.

Again and again, our theme is ACTION. To accomplish a program, do the following:

Experiential learning should:

~ Spark imaginations and Challenge Intellects
~ Allow the Visitor to Become Part of the Action
~ Provide Personal Accomplishment and Growth
~ Protect Natural & Cultural Heritage Resources
~ Promote Appreciation and Enjoyment
~ Respect Host Community Rights and Values

Humans respond to LOVE: the basis of Christianity. It is too bad that English has only one word to describe it. Ancient Greek had four:

1. Agape: deep unconditional, selfless love (used in the Bible to express God's love for us)
2. Eros: romantic, physical or sexual love (hence the term erotic)
3. Philia: brotherly love or friendship (such as Philadelphia, the city of brother love)

4. Storge: affection; empathy bond (used primarily to describe family relationships)

Agape is the status Titus wants all souls to reach. Heretics will divert people often for their own personal gain. You will read this but can you act on it??? In trying to build a new system, use these tools:

   a. Many things that are desirable are not feasible.
   b. Individuals and communities face trade-offs.
   c. Other people have more information about their abilities, their efforts, and their preferences than you do.
   d. Everyone responds to incentives, including people you want to help. That is why social safety nets don't always end up working as intended.
   e. It is feasible for one generation to shift costs to subsequent ones. That is what national government debts and the U.S. social security system do.
   f. When a government transfers money, its citizens eventually pay, either today or tomorrow, either through explicit taxes or implicit ones like inflation.
   g. People want other people to pay for them. Heretics will make false promises. They will use pride, lust, greed and envy to attack followers and divide the flock.

Selecting future leaders is the MOST difficult task you will face. People are the rock you will build your life upon. Be careful, you must be strong enough to turn away many who will waste your time and squander your resources. Like Titus, have a plan and follow it.

`As an example of how heretics have diverted that value of people's resources, review the following chart to see how the value of your dollars have been radically reduced:

The Rise In The US M2 Money Supply And Federal Reserve Bank Balance Sheet

Data sources:
https://fred.stlouisfed.org/series/M2 and
https://fred.stlouisfed.org/series/WALCL

M2 Money Supply Chg from 9/16/2019
(amounts in billions of dollars)

9/16/2019	$14,990.4	—-
12/30/2019	$15,328.2	+2.3%
2/24/2020	$15,508.2	+3.5%
9/28/2020	$18,652.6	+24.4%

Federal Reserve Balance Sheet
              Chg from 9/11/2019
(amounts in billions of dollars)

9/11/2019	$3,769.673	—-
1/1/2020	$4,173.626	+10.7%
2/19/2020	$4,171.570	+10.7%
10/7/2020	$7,085.369	+88.0%

Source:U.S. Government

It is not the strongest or the most intelligent who will survive but those who can best manage change.

HEBREWS & JAMES

The biblical version deals with the source of Temptation, futility of creed, without conduct. It deals with the inconsistency of undue deference to "rich" men. When faith does NOT produce good works, it is spurious. A common theme is valuing patience and God power to supply power for good conduct and control of your tongue. Hebrews makes it perfectly clear that Jesus is superior to angels. Moses' laws are a servant to Jesus. Now we have a new covenant based on love with God. Now I give you tools to accomplish James' goals.

This book uses these examples to expose our weakness.

The Golden Rule of investing is to "cut your losses short and let your winners ride." Nearly every successful investor on the planet abides by this rule – however, there are very few successful investors who regularly beat the markets.

For example, consider the following results of faith dealing with risk:

"Imagine that a rare disease is breaking out and is expected to kill 600 people. Two different programs are available to deal with the threat. If Program 1 is adopted, 200 people will be saved. It is risky because 400 will die using procedure 2. A procedure that patient people (with a creed that all life matters) is adopted, there is a 33% probability that everyone will be saved and a 67% probability that no one will be saved.

"Which program would you choose? If most of us are risk-averse, rational people will prefer Plan 1's certainty of saving 200 lives over Plan B's gamble. 72% of people chose the risk-averse response represented by Plan 1 while only 28% were for Plan 2.

The explanation the researchers give for this is that people are not risk averse: they are perfectly willing to choose a gamble when they consider it appropriate. However, they are loss averse...

James' message is that we are not as rational as we think we are. What we are is loss averse. We don't want to take a loss. However, if we are to succeed in life, we must learn to take a loss, and take it early: because a small loss can't be allowed to become a catastrophic loss.

You have to force yourself to go against what probably feels natural. You need to learn to cut losses early, and you need to learn to let winners ride. Put simply, the way you build self-confidence is to combine a few small losses with big winners.

In order to win the war, you've got to learn to concede some battles. You've got to admit you're wrong sometimes. Follow these simple rules and develop a habit of winning friends and letting your faith produce good works:

1. Be sympathetic with the other person's fears and desires.
2. Begin all conversations in a friendly way.
3. Get the other person to say "yes" as soon as possible.
4. Never say, "You're wrong."
5. Never get yourself into an argument.
6. When wrong, admit it immediately.

7. Let the other person feel that your idea is his own.

Live an honest life filled with wholesome experiences, then your being will enjoy warm memories of the past and shiny dreams for the future.

PETER I, II

MISINFORMATION

In Rome, Peter offered new hope on his vision of salvation, realization of the Jewish prophets and assurance of the Gospel based on seeing Jesus alive and witnessing the mystery of transfiguration. The early church had no organized priesthood or discipline. Many of the earlier followers were slaves and women who yearned for purpose in their lives and hoping for anything after death. Because the foundation was Jewish, Peter based his writing on justifying the Hebrew Torah. Breaking from the Jewish tribal blood lines and opening up a simple but direct pathway to God (cutting out the rabbi and "system" led to many false teachers and problems). Many were traitors to the Roman culture causing additional pressure between passive resistance and upright revolt. (Most followers did not have the means to physically resist so they were not punished when Titus the Roman emperor in 70 A.D. decided to finally end the "Jewish" problem and destroyed the temple, gutting Jerusalem and selling the Jews into slavery.)

This book does NOT deal with the spiritual life, but rather shows modern policies that exploit today's population with false teachings and outdated policies protecting the elites who will do anything to keep power rather than promote the experimental American way of a ladder to greater personal happiness.

These are some of those policies:

1. False: Meat is necessary.

A diet high in nitrogenous meats and proteins, along with other acids that come directly from food, combines with the acidic residues of muscular activity, causing acidic wastes to predominate. Meat causes calcium (an alkaline mineral) to be pulled from the bones as a buffer. Natural sulfur is also required to neutralize the poisons resulting from digestion. Indol, one of the degradation products of animal cells, requires an enormous amount of sulfur for neutralization. Since sulfur is also necessary for the fixation of calcium, using the body's sulfur stores for neutralizing animal products is disastrous for calcification of the bones.

2. False: Take more drugs to be well.

Compounding the problem are drugs that wipe out friendly intestinal bacteria that destroy uric acid and other metabolic wastes. These drugs include not only antibiotics, which kill friendly and unfriendly bacteria indiscriminately. Aspirin prevents the reproduction of bacteria, including those that detoxify uric acid. Cortisone and its derivative have many other harmful effects. Antiseptics and certain chemicals in commercial foods also destroy beneficial bacteria.

EPISTLE OF JOHN AND JUDE

Like many of the letters in the New Testament, John gives a definition of life as practical obedience to God's rules. God is the light giving a commendation of hospitality and brotherly kindness. Jude believed that even those ungodly people have found a place in the church.

The letter also raises strong denunciation of unworthy members and false teachers. This book takes this message and exposes the government and food companies' false teachings on the safety of processed FOOD. See five (5) FDA chemicals to avoid.(In my opinion, the FDA stated the amounts allowed in food that I do not believe.)

1. **FDA Approved #1: Hydrogenated Oils** are added to food to increase shelf life, and are also found in crackers, cookies, salad dressings, and bread. The oils are made by bubbling hydrogen gas into vats of liquid vegetable oil-as the hydrogen binds to the oil's free

carbon atoms, it solidifies and creates Trans fats, which have been shown to contribute to increased risk of cardiovascular disease.

2. **FDA Approved #2: Aspartame** is an artificial sweetener—brand names are Equal and NutraSweet—that also appears to be an excitotoxin and may cause nerve damage.

3. **FDA Approved #3: Sodium Nitrate** is found in processed meats such as bacon, ham, corned beef and hot dogs and increases the risk of pancreatic cancer. Solution: Have some bacon now and then—the saturated fat is good for you—but generally, stick to unprocessed meats.

4. **FDA Approved #4: High Fructose Corn Syrup (HFCS)** is one of the major drivers of the obesity epidemic. It's everywhere. Americans today take in an average of 55 pounds per year—an estimated one-sixth of daily calories! It is incredibly cheap to make adding $$$ for the food industry. It ratchets up your taste buds to require more food.

5. **FDA Approved #5: Monosodium glutamate (MSG)** is a classic excitotoxin, which means it stimulates cells to the point of damage or death. Brain cells are particularly vulnerable. MSG may cause brain damage.

Food companies ADD chemicals to increase sales. For example, here are foods to avoid:

1. **Food to Avoid #1: Preservatives BHA (butylated hydroxyanisole) and BHT (butylated**

hydroxytoluene) are common preservatives, found in breakfast cereals, nut mixes, chewing gum, butter-substitute spreads, processed meats, dehydrated potatoes, and beer.

2. **Food to Avoid #2: Milk and Dairy Products With rBGH (recombinant bovine growth hormone)** is the largest selling dairy animal drug in America. Commercial dairy operators inject it into cows to increase milk production. But it may present multiple dangers to human health including a possibility of increased risk of cancer.

3. **Food to Avoid #3: Foods with Artificial Food Colors and Dyes:** A dizzying—in some cases, literally—3,000 food additives are included in American processed foods. These preservatives, flavorings, colors, and other ingredients are especially common in foods targeted at young children—whose developing nervous systems are particularly vulnerable to their effects. Protect your grandchildren.

4. **Food to Avoid #4: Arsenic-Laced Chicken**: Incredibly, arsenic-based drugs are approved for use in animal feed in the U.S. Why? Because they make animals grow faster and their meat appear pinker, creating the illusion that old meat is fresh. The FDA contends these products are safe because they contain "organic arsenic", which is less toxic than the other, inorganic form, which is a known carcinogen.

5. **Food to Avoid #5: Bread With Potassium Bromate**: "Bromated" flour contains potassium bromated, an oxidizing agent widely used in commercial baking—it

strengthens and improves dough and promotes rising. Concerns about bromated flour go all the way back to 1982, when research suggested that the chemical causes several types of cancer in lab rats.

6. **Food to Avoid #6: Olestra/Olean**: Synthetic fats are commercially produced substitutes for the real thing. They provide fewer calories or no calories at all. The best known of these is olestra, known by the trademarked name Olean and approved by the FDA in 1996. This synthetic oil passes through the digestive tract without being digested or absorbed. Sounds like the ultimate glutton fantasy—eat junk food endlessly, gain no weight. It does NOT work well and should be avoided.

To be healthier, raise your own food or buy organic. If you cannot find or afford organic, follow EWG's guides:

The fifteen cleanest foods are: Avocados, sweet corn, pienappple, onions, papaya, sweet peas, eggplants, asparagus, cauliflower, cantalope, broccoli, mushrooms, cabbage, honeydew melon, kiwi;

The 2020 Dirty Dozen List are: Strawberries, spinach, kale, nectarines, apples, grapes, peaches, cherie, pears, tomaatoes, celery, potatoes.

These foods are those that nutritionists eat every day: tea, ginger, olives, Brussel sprouts, flaxseed, walnut pesto, hemp seeds, apple cider vinegar with the mother, watermelon water, chia seeds, quinoa, amaranth, sweet potatoes, swiss chard, goji berries, kale, jackfruit, wild salmon, nut milk-based cream cheese, dandelion greens, chickpea pasta, coconut oil, broccoli, butternut squash, cucumber, and hummus.

Inflammation is NOT all bad. It is the system to fight bacteria and bad microbes in your body. If stress causes it to escape its normal bounds, you should avoid GMO foods, sugars and eat raw extra virgin olive oils. (Use avocado or coconut oil for cooking as high heat oxidizes EVOO.)

In summary, avoid processed foods, eat organic and get hungry now and then. Give your digestive system a chance to rest. It will calm the body and reduce the blood markers for inflammation.

REVELATIONS

It was written by an old man James, brother of Jesus, when he was in bitter exile. It provides a mystic, wild vision of the second coming. For fifty years, the Christians prepared for the second coming that did NOT come. This book changed the narrative and provided hope that in the future, Christ would save the good and destroy the evil. It provided how judgments would hold people accountable for their SINS. It used a massive arrangement of seals, trumpets and vials. It contains vivid stories of a sun-crowned woman persecuted by a dragon and two wild beasts. In short, it provided cover for the teachers and later the priesthood to hold "secrets" of the future happenings.

In this book, we state a simple prophecy of what we can.

Because of technology, human behavior has become more specialized. This means in the short term, productivity has increased and the standard of living has improved. All of this leads people to be more dependent upon the government that has used the internet and monetary controls to dictate the narrative to society. In turn, this leads to more socialistic programs and governmental interference that will continue to reduce the individual and tribal constraints in society.

In the future when nature or weather causes a massive disruption in the mechanized society, people who have lost their ability to feed, clothe and shelter themselves will panic and a dark age of misery and death will immerge.

Science will expand until an unintended consequence of its research causes an unintended mutation in the societal fabric. The result will be further misery, death and a transformation of society. Technology will continue to be rapidly embraced by people all of the world, but the cultural behavior will not keep up with the robotic and artificial intelligence potential. This struggle will end in conflict and the destruction of civilization as we know it.

What do you see? One, two or three pictures?

The pessimist complains about the wind; the optimist expects it to change; the realist adjusts the sails.--- --William Arthur Ward

O God, give us the grace to live worthily and to hold our inheritance as a sacred trust, that we may leave it increased, for those who shall come after. Amen

PART III

A Road Away from Hell

Call L. Bruckner for coaching and questions, 815-259-3168
or bruck175@hotmail.com

INTRODUCTION TO PART III

TIMES HAVE CHANGED OR HAVE THEY???

Since WWII, the narrative of society has changed. With electricity, transistors, computers, medicines, chemical farming and diverse energy sources of energy, people have become more and more specialized. The benefits have greatly increased productivity and the short term standard of living. Coupled with a peace dividend (stop destroying people and things), it has become better to invest and work to improve one's tribe then steal from others. (Will the population explosion and hunger force us back to stealing from others causing war?)

The primary motive of human existence is to avoid PAIN, whether it is physical, social, mental or spiritual. Mankind has endeavored to avoid pain by becoming more specialized. We have created more supply and reduced the causes of pain. A huge population increase has used this increased supply resulting from peace (security). Innovated technologies and discoveries reduce demand. This dramatic change in life-style and abundance has a dark side. Absolute truth has caved into moral pluralism. What was considered endorsed perversion is now encouraged as alternative lifestyles. We've rewarded laziness and corruption in a welfare system (Romans use bread and circus).

We have condemned and exploited the poor and called it a lottery. The powerful, well connected have used the economic game (called capitalism until now they have all the marbles and pulled up the ladders to achieve the American dream of private ownership. It protects their wealth for their use and their children.

By inverting our value system, we failed to discipline our children and called it building self- esteem. Instead of stealing our neighbor's possessions, we accomplish it with ever increasing taxes. We have polluted the air (internet) with pornography and disrespectful profanity and called it freedom of expression. In the education cabal, we have removed studying of our family and local communities' history and traditions. We added further abuse by ridiculing the time-honored values of our forefathers and called it enlightenment. We have assaulted the value of life. In the name of choice, we kill the unborn and then perversely kill the abortionist in the name of "right to life".

Everything has changed so quickly with the specialization of work that people do not know what they do not know. Because we have forsaken the basic skills of living, we are now more dependent on others for our needs. This dependency is forced upon us by government using fear, class warfare and printing fake dollars (FIAT currency backed by nothing except your TRUST in the central government).

Western civilization has become faceless (internet) and soulless. While we are 'expert' at our specialty, we added tremendous value to mankind, but in concentrating our efforts in perfecting our craft, we lost individual freedoms, thought and accountability. Laziness has morphed into political correctness. To get along, we go along, not seeing the long- term price of unintended consequences (soil depletion, global warming).

This treatise <u>Roadmap Away From Hell for Seniors</u> will provide insight to help you move away from the misery of Hell. You must take ACTION AND NEVER GIVE UP if you want to take the first step on the road to peace and harmony with Nature. PLEASE, THINK. Many think they are thinking when they are merely rearranging their prejudices. Remember Big Brother is watching. DO NOT LOVE BIG BROTHER!!!

WHY PEOPLE FEAR RETIREMENT

Many people fear retirement for the following reasons:

- (26%) One illness will wipe out your financial security. Although Medicare and Obamacare have changed the equation, there are still risks. **Solution**: It is vital to have a good Medicare supplement policy. Stay with a known company. Do not carry overlapping policies, i.e. cancer, accident, heart. Get three opinions and quotes. Get Part D; every month you do not have a drug plan increases your costs due to the penalty.

— Suffocating inactivity and boredom. What am I going to do with myself? Solution: Assess your skills and talents. Join a service club, church, community group. BE PROACTIVE. Develop a hobby, go to the gym, join classes, exercise, etc.

— (18%) Because of a high cost of living, many pack up and move. Picking the wrong place can be depressing. **Solution**: Rent before you buy. Consider whether you want to be close to family and old friends or do you want better weather. Consider the following criteria:

— Low cost of living (it's low for a reason)

— Do they have special services for seniors—be specific

— What are the cultural and recreational options?

— What is the average temperature (55 degrees with 55% humidity)? Don't go to Houston if you do not want rain, swamp and hurricanes!

— What are the housing, food, and transportation costs?

— What are the medical facilities; check cost and quality

— (23%) Fear: What if your investment/bank collapses and you cannot recover (you need to diversify, make sure your bank is FDIC insured.)

— (5%) Taxes and inflation will destroy their standard of living. **Solution:** BUY NOW! What do you think you will need for life? Exhaust taxable savings before using deferred IRA and 401K funds.

— (5%) Having plenty of money but too little income. Solution: use reverse mortgage, liquidate some stocks and keep a cash reserve at home.

- (23%) NOT enough money to live on? Here is where planning when you are 40 allows time to build reserves, diversity and grow using compound interest.
- Losing it all. **Solution**: Have real assets like land, apartments, gold and cash. Diversify; never put more than 10% in any one asset class. Never more than 40% in stocks; look for alternative investments like estate tax certificates, collectables, gold, jewelry, farm land or timber, SAFE 401K, IRA (you can have two (2) at the same time: a regular IRA and a Roth IRA ($6,000 limit to $6000 per worker husband and wife if both worked. Look at the next two pages; discuss with family and fill in expenses, then have the discipline to follow the plan.

TAKE AWAY: Remember

- Have at least three (3) kinds of retirement money.
- Watch wealth investments as closely as you monitor business income and family budget.
- Plan NOW your pleasures, profits and portfolio. It is a pathway away from Hell.
- Calculate your needs with REAL HARD numbers.
- DO NOT just SIT and HOLD ON. On your birthday and on January 1, discuss a written plan for where you have been, where you are NOW, and what you should change to make next year better. NO ONE CARES about your welfare more than you do. Don't stress, plan and enjoy the ride. You only get one.

ROADMAP

As you draw and review your roadmap to avoid the pathway to Hell, here are factors you may have forgotten to consider.

- Is there enough cushion between what ought to happen and what can happen? Many times a spouse will agree to a restructuring and then NOT do it. This causes fights, shortfalls and depression. Be careful about your spouse and your children's interests. Often their sense of "entitlement" leads to families not talking to each other and destroying family bonds.
- Check social security, pensions, life insurance, wills, trusts, annuities, etc. READ them. Have your children understand them so they can execute them when you are sick or dead.
- If you are caretaking for someone in the family, do NOT forget to care for your own health and well being.

In ten (10) years, can you handle ALL the details, the house, the car, the doctors, the community, your parents, your children, etc.?

- How are you going to handle grief? Is therapy available? Who is going to fill the holes in your family life?

- Too many roadmaps start tomorrow. You must spell out clear action NOW. Reduce TV or computer time NOW. If you do not need everything you currently have, gift money and things NOW. See how the recipient enjoys or wastes your assets. Start using your hands (get crafty). Remember the 4-H pledge: I pledge my HEAD to clearer thinking, my HEART to greater loyalty, my HANDS to larger service, and my HEALTH to better living, for my club, my community, my country, and my world. All four need to be used NOW. Your journey of a thousand miles starts with a simple step TODAY.

- Walk; stay active. In your roadmap, structure your days. Participate in free senior classes, reach out to new contacts, or take a cruise. You don't need one "big" job, just many small projects. Travel early in your retirement. DO NOT put off as your health may start failing making traveling painful (bad knees, poor hearing or eyesight, constipation, etc.).

- Consolidate your assets, allocate by diversifying but not too much. If you have a business, what is the succession Plan A, Plan B. There will be difficult conversations about housing, money, pets, and children. Don't forget the tax advisor.

- Do you want to live in a retirement community, full spectrum facilities, college environment, city or country, one story or two, house or apartment, own or rent? Do you really want to move to Portugal, Costa Rica, Panama, Uruguay, or Vietnam??? Rent before you buy.

- Do you really need a life coach or financial advisor? Honestly, look at your track record. If you did not save or have not earned at least 5% in annual growth, you NEED professional help. Invest carefully; be wary of annuities, hidden fees or a broker who lives on commission. Is he a fiduciary for YOU or his own family?
- Are you driving the safest car you can afford? Life is valuable.
- Where are your valuables? Are they safe? Use a deposit box, fire proof safe, or a tin can under the dog house. Let two people you can trust know the location, source and value. Is the painting worth $50 or$5000? Make sure they know how to maximize the value of the assets, coins, etc.
- Economize without changing your lifestyle. Read books and buy used.
- You do not have to retire 100%, maybe part time. Start a home business or turn a hobby into something more. It takes time to write, revise, reflect, discuss, reread, review and change annually. Good luck!

REMEMBER TO KEEP NEEDS SMALL: PLANNING A $900 FUNERAL

When a loved one dies, the last thing you want to worry about is money. Funeral directors, like attorneys, are just waiting to "help" you when you are at your most vulnerable. Funerals today are averaging between $7,000 and $10,000. Funerals with cremation run $6,000 to $7,000. This includes viewing and burial, basic service fees, transporting remains to a funeral home, a casket, embalming and other preparation. Insurance salesmen are constantly trolling senior citizens trying to sell "peace of mind" burial policies. Beware before you get suckered in: Plan, Prepare, and ACT now to save later.

You do not need to go into debt to honor a loved one. By choosing cremation and exercising creativity, thousands of dollars can be saved.

Plan ahead: talking about death is NEVER fun or easy but necessary. Does he want to be cremated quickly with no ceremony or does the loved one want a large funeral with all the whistles and bells? The funeral industry is trying to sell you expensive options. See Karen Leonard's research of "The American Way of Death Revisited" by Jessica Mitford.

Start with the FTC brochure "Funeral: A Consumer Guide" and the website provided by Funeral Consumers Alliance: https://funerals.org/

Shop around; prices vary widely. Thousands of dollars can be saved. Select "direct cremation"; no embalmment is required. Make sure the cost of direct cremation is included in the actual crematory fee (several hundreds of dollars).

Rent or buy a simple casket. Buying a $5,000 fancy gilded casket for a body soon to be burned to ashes is stupid.

Avoid an expensive urn; use a cardboard or plastic box instead. If you want to display the urn, buy your own tasteful piece of pottery.

Use a church, service hall, park, art gallery for a "Celebration of Life" event instead of paying big bucks to the funeral home. Have parties before someone dies.

Be smart and use photo albums, diplomas, favorite foods, golf clubs, baseball gloves, etc. instead of expensive lavish flowers (that die anyway) to decorate your area.

Hold a birthday or anniversary memorial instead of a funeral; this may allow more people to attend.

Hold a service anywhere: your house, the beach, a park, a lodge, any place that was special to the loved one. Allow everyone attending to share their stories and memories.

Plant a tree or put up a bench somewhere meaningful to you and/or your loved one. Check out "The Living Urn" or other bio urns on the market.

Join a memorial society for information and discounts. Check out nonprofit organizations for package deals.

If you do want a direct cremation (there is no public viewing of the body), there is no need for embalming. View your loved one privately.

Shop for a modest casket. Check the Web. Bury your loved one in their favorite clothes and skip new clothes. Use grave liners and vaults. Do not get pressured into buying a burial vault. Check with cemetery requirements. Dig your own hole for a cremation urn and save the digging fee. On monuments, check the Web; you will be shocked by the variation in prices.

Check for help, especially the Veterans Administration. Social Security offers a onetime death benefit of $255 payable to the spouse or children. Check pension, societies and churches that defray funeral expenses.

Be very cautious about pre- paying funeral expenses; Illinois lost all the money one time. Finally, donate your body to science. If done right, the medical research or school will pay all expenses.

2020 SPECIFIC SUGGESTIONS FOR SENIORS

Investing is difficult. Brokers will break you. They are salesmen, selling, selling, and selling. The 607 billionaires and thousands of millionaires in the USA are not going to allow the system to change because the system is how they made their money. The industrial/defense complex is also going to continue creating war. One reason Obama/Trump were successful in reducing unemployment is that all the military equipment had to be manufactured in the USA.

Today, the stock market (September 2020) is too high because the privately owned federal reserve bank is printing money out of thin air and pumping up to $500,000,000 a month into supporting 2%-4% real estate loans and junk corporate bonds. The reason the bank is doing this is because corporations and the wealthy do not want deflation. It would lead to a depression. If people know prices will drop, they will stop buying now and wait for the prices to go lower.

Because of this fear, the government will try to inflate the economy with cheaper dollars. When this happens, you want real assets: gold, silver, real estate and some stocks. Consider the following: American Express AXP, Apple AAPL, Coca-Cola KO, Home Depot HD, Johnson & Johnson JNJ, McDonald's MCD, Microsoft MSFT, Proctor & Gamble PG, UPS, Walmart WMT, PayPal PYPL, Square SQ, Global Payments GPN, York Water Company YORW, Assurant AIZP, Waste Management WM, CME Group CME, Buffalo Small Cap Fund BUFSX, or Vanguard Total Stock Market Index Fund VTI.

If you want to speculate, contact Lending Club, LC. and see how you can loan money to businesses and earn 6-20% on your investment.

If you want to work and earn 10% to 15% per year, investigate buying delinquent tax liens at the county courthouse. Illinois is having the second highest average real estate tax and an investor friendly auction. Illinois and Arizona are two of the best states to buy liens.

We are in a stock market bubble; too much demand for too little stock raises prices and creates a "wealth effect". No one knows when the elite will pull the punch bowl. Think of the stock market as ice frozen in a leaky bucket. The "deep state" at some point will put a fire under the bucket. When the 20-degree frozen ice reaches 32 degrees, the solid ice will turn to water and the leaky bucket will drain the wealth into the hands of those who started the fire.

Ninety-nine percent of Americans are not feasting on cheap money. Disposable income has fallen. In 2007, the typical household was worth $142,000. In 2017, it drops to around $56,000. Even before Medicare or government subsidized student loans, 40 million Americans were receiving food stamps in 2017 (Rome 'bread and circuses'). An estimated 59 million are on welfare and over 13 million are on unemployment. Government transfers money from workers to welfare and subsidies. In 1960, 10% of the money transferred went to welfare, now it is over 35%. Medical costs, tuition, housing costs have all skyrocketed. Now asset inflation has added fuel to the fire to melt the ice bucket and enrich the privileged. Consider the above factors when drawing your roadmap. Potterville is becoming a reality. % slavery is next in a Brave New Normal.

It will be impossible to stop the downward slope when socialism has 62% of the population gets some form of federal government money. Demand inflation raged in the 1970-1980s when baby boomers started families, bought houses, cars, furniture, etc. Today the USA is aging Americans, of which there are millions and whose numbers rise by 10,000 turning 65 per day. That rate of retiree growth will continue for at least another decade and a half.

Now, we're not saying that these folks are not due those payments. But it does raise the question of where the money will come from when millions upon millions of newly retired Americans suddenly sign up for retirement benefits.

After Social Security and Medicare, national defense is next in the budget at 16%, then welfare programs at 10%. Interest payments alone on our debt—not paying a cent of the actual debt itself!—are 6% of your tax dollar, even with interest rates at nearly zero. Imagine what will happen when interest rates rise back to "ordinary" levels or worse when inflation causes the bond market to collapse? Japan and China will stop buying bonds and use dollars to buy assets. Earlier I stated asset inflation is going up. Where will gold, silver, and land values be when asset inflation is 10%, or MORE??? How high can taxes go? Who will pay for the free lunch started in 2007?

In your roadmap,. Be able to grow your own food. Plan what you need until death. Build a survival box. Learn basic skills. Move to the country. All of the above are options to consider in drawing up a roadmap away from the hell the elites have built here on earth. They are even causing global warming so it feels like Hell!

That's where we are today...where once again Big Government and the economy it created is desperately struggling to survive.

We are a nation with a government that's deeply in debt (due to the Republicans mishandling of the budget), with a rapidly depreciating currency and a banking system that nearly imploded only a few years ago.

And the Feds recognize that despite a booming stock market, we're still $806,160 in debt per US family plus new debt caused by the Covid-19 Virus. The Federal Government sees that the number of Americans willing to work is stuck near a 38-year low...and that 94 million Americans are not in the labor force...that is BEFORE the virus struck. This problem will be compounded in the future as robots and technology reduce the human workforce. They understand that stocks are overvalued except for the dot-com collapse. Who knows how long they continue to inflate the balloon before the balloon bursts. The government can not indefinitely keep stealing from the future with more debt and still remain the world's reserve currency.

HEALTH IS OUR NUMBER ONE PRIORITY

I. An ounce of prevention is worth a pound of cure. You are what you eat. Strive to consume a whole food plant-based diet avoiding refined sugars and starches, processed foods, and excessive caffeinated and alcoholic beverages. Eat the rainbow of fruits and vegetables and the good fats like avocados, extra virgin olive oil, nuts and seeds, fatty fish, whole eggs and dark chocolate.

II. Make the body strong by exercising 150 minutes per week to stimulate the lymphatic system including resistance training.

III. Use good habits: daily movement, good eating, restful sleep, clean living.

IV. Aging: utilize meditation and yoga.

V. Balances: Chinese philosophy of Ying/Yang; reduce stress NOW with deep breathing

VI. Water: get a home filter system to remove unwanted chemicals and add magnesium

VII. Sunshine: aim to get 10-30 minutes per day to make Vitamin D

VIII. Malnutrition can be caused by too little or too much of certain nutrients; balance is the key.

IX. Protections/Preventions
   A. Echinacea to help fight infections
   B. Take a good multivitamin from organic source without chemicals to supplement your healthy diet
   C. Mineral deficiencies:
      1. Zinc to reduce inflammation
      2. Sea Salt for minerals
      3. Magnesium to help your heart, muscles and immune system function properly
      4. Selenium to help with metabolism and thyroid function
      5. Iron binds with hemoglobin and gets oxygen to your cells; use food sources

X. Arthritis Pain can be relieved by adding turmeric (with black pepper) to your foods

XI. Use aromatherapy and music to build up your immune system

XII. Common treatments include using extra virgin olive oil, apple cider vinegar with the mother, ginger and garlic

XIII. Air pollution is killing you. Plant ferns inside your house will filter the air, remove CO_2 and convert sugars into oxygen. More music plants and less electromagnetic energy in NATURE is best.

Observe YOUR body cycles, use them to determine when to fast, eat, sleep defecate, study or exercise.

No one cares about your health like you do. The following is a simple outline for seniors. Because we have depleted our soil and poisoned our food with chemicals, we have weakened our body. Adding dead water and air pollution, Americans are being killed! Do not trust the drug companies and their pills to provide short term cures. Be like the Chinese who base medicine on what you eat and drink. Longevity factors include:

Try following the GBOMBS Diet (Dr Joel Fuhrman: <u>The End of Dieting: How to Live for Life</u>):

G Greens: powerful antioxidant, promotes healthy vision, prevents diabetes and anti cancer

B Beans: satisfy protein and carb requirements with resistant starch to prevent colon issues

O Onions: Chop and chew to start a chemical reaction which helps reduce inflammation

M Mushrooms: binds and labels abnormal cells so the immune system can destroy them

B Berries (& pomegranates): Antioxidants with the highest nutrient-to-calorie ratio of any fruit
S Seeds: Prevent fat from being absorbed, pulls bad fats out of bloodstream to be removed

Use sunshine and water to regulate the body. When you fail to build up the immune system, the following will help after you reduce stress and inflammation.

Detox your liver by eating garlic, beets, organic apples, broccoli spouts, watermelon, fermented foods, walnuts and avocado.

Detox your body by limiting alcohol, focus on sleep, drink plenty of water (64 oz per day), reduce your intake of sugar and processed foods, eat antioxidant-rich foods, eat foods high in prebiotics (i.e. fiber), decrease your salt intake, get active, eat sulfur-containing foods (onions, broccoli, garlic), try out chlorella, flavor dishes with cilantro, support glutathione (eggs, broccoli, garlic), switch to natural cleaning products and choose natural body care products.

There are ways to prevent or reduce diabetes: cut out sugar and refined carbs, work out regularly, drink water as your primary beverage, lose weight if you're overweight or obese, quit smoking, follow a very-low carb diet, watch portion sizes and avoid sedentary behaviors, eat a high-fiber diet, optimize vitamin D, eliminate processed foods, drink coffee and tea (green is the best due to EGCG), and add natural herbs to your diet (curcumin, berberine, cinnamon).

You only have one body, so stay safe!

See chart below to get an estimate of the cost of NOT taking care of your body.

HEALTH

Anual Pre-Retirement Healthcare Cost Based on Health Management

Age	Health is Poorly Managed	Health is Well Managed	Health Care Savings
45	$5,974	$4,424	$1,550
50	$8,598	$6,339	$2,259
55	$12,850	$9,372	$3,478
60	$17,335	$12,726	$4,609
64	$21,095	$15,691	$5,404
Total	$254,887	$187,456	$67,431
Average	$12,744	$9,373	$3,371

Source: Medicare: U.S. Government

Support the secret endocannabinoid with wild salmon, walnuts, avocados while avoiding anything that has phthalates chemicals, i.e., hairspray, perfumes. To get an extra boost try raw kale, krill oil, blueberries, broccoli, spinach, carrots, onions, cayenne peppers, beets, cinnamon, vinegar, sauerkraut, organic eggs, beans, and yogurts.

All sickness, all diseases and ultimately death is the result of the aggressive accumulations of toxin (poison) in the blood and body. In western society, the drug business has commercialized solving one problem that causes other problems. Your body and telomeres will finally stop reproducing new cells. In essence, you will starve to death and die.

HEALTH HABITS: YOU ARE WHAT YOU EAT

HERE ARE MORE WAYS TO STAY HEALTHY

If you do NOT want to use your health insurance, you need sound health habits in addition to good sleep, 150 minutes of exercise per week, daily sunlight or vitamin D supplement, daily self massage and you need to eat right. Listed are foods you should eat with "live" water to drink and/or green tea.

Eat organic: fruits (apple per day, avocados, blueberries, dates, kiwi, tomatoes), vegetables (beans, cabbage, carrots, celery, cucumbers, garlic, ginger, leafy greens, mushrooms, onions, potatoes, spinach, sweet potatoes), nuts and seeds including chia and flax seeds, whole grains including organic old fashioned or steel cut oatmeal, wild caught salmon, sardines, mackerel and herring, spices like black pepper, cinnamon, curcumin/turmeric, and sea salt, whole milk and yogurt.

Eat prebiotics to stimulate the growth of healthy bacteria in the gut; fruits, vegetables, fiber.

Here's a healthy drink: Haymaker's Punch or Switchel (mix and enjoy!)

2 quarts water
½ cup apple cider vinegar

¾ teaspoon organic honey
½ Tablespoon ginger

Keep your body alkaline. Stay away from acidic and processed foods, excess simple carbohydrates, excessive alcohol and excessive caffeine.

If over 40 years of age, eat the following:
Curcumin (found in turmeric and activates certain proteins and protects against cellular damage),
EGCG and Theanine (green tea intake helps restore mitochondrial function in cells),
Collagen (powders and capsules may prevent skin aging),
CoQ10 (reduces oxidative stress),
Rhodiola (anti-inflammatory),
Garlic (prevents skin aging and wrinkles),
Astragalus (reduces oxidative stress, promotes immune function and prevents cellular damage) and
Resveratrol (grapes, berries, peanuts and red wine for longevity).

Other essential supplements include:
Omega-3s for heart health, immune functioning, brain health and inflammatory response axthanthin for the eyes
Probiotics to enhance immune function help with digestive tract infections and promote good digestion
Vitamin D3 regulates calcium and phosphorus as well as insulin

ESSENTIAL IMMUNITY

In another section, I discuss the steps needed to maintain a vital immune system. There is a more basic truth that is hidden from you by a powerful, corrupt, profit driven drug industry. Allopathic medicine is sickness NOT wellness. Your healthcare professionals treat symptoms and diseases using drugs, radiation, or surgery. Driven by profits, it must have sick people to consume drugs. Often developing more sickness requires different drugs like "pain killers" and yes, they will kill you sooner or later. The government has little interest in preventive medicine. Immunizations do not insure wellness. Life can never come from death.

The real fork in the road develops between Antoine Béchamp (1816-1908) and Louis Pasteur (1822-1895). Béchamp believed that the ongoing disease is within the body not outside. The condition of the immune system determined why and how a person recovered. Basically using the premiere of Eastern medicine, he concluded humans create their own microbes to balance life. He also isolated microzymas (smallest living particles). Germs actually help activate the particles to become healthy microbes to heal the organs.

Pasteur claimed illness was caused by external pathogens. Bad microbes had one purpose and always caused the same disease. Béchamp had proven the opposite; the body can create its own microorganisms in order to re-establish order and balance in the body. An entire book could be written about the battle between microzymas changing shape (pleomorphism) versus monomorphism. You need to study the difference between using synthetic chemical pharmaceuticals and building an immune system to heal yourself. To keep your current cells alive take dimethyl glum(DMG). The chemical DMG supports the transformation of calcium lactate converting it to calcium bicarbonate. It is iodized by vitamin D that puts it into the blood stream through your intestines, while Vitamin C promotes phagocytosis that increases the oxygen capacity carrying of the blood.

Fat soluble Vitamin A plus C helps prevent visual infections. After consuming the above omega3 fatty acids and linotenic acid are converted in the liver.

When you have a well rested body, proper exercise and an alkaline diet, the four horsemen will maximize the oxygen transfer more efficiently. Your blood pressure will drop, your heart and lungs do not have to work so hard supplying the necessary glucose and oxygen to the millions of hungry cells.

Secret: The truth is you do not lose energy because you age; you age because lose energy.

SENIOR IMMUNE BOOSTERS

For seniors, adding Myrrh, Black Cumin Seed Oil and Oregano Oil will enhance your immune system.

Eat chicken soup: The broth releases the amino acid cysteine that activates your T cells.

Natural yogurt helps keep your intestinal tract clean of sickness caused by bad bacteria and germs.

Fibrin is a fibrous, non-globular protein involved in the clotting of blood and is involved in arthritis and joint inflammation. Undigested food particles and microbes pass too easily into the bloodstream, which is known as leaky gut. These foreign bodies are considered bad and cause the fibrin to fight. The battle causes inflammation and swelling resulting in the PAIN and swelling of arthritis. To reduce inflammation, eat curry (turmeric), and ginger, take bromelain, boswellia extract and white willow bark (it contains salicin, a chemical similar to aspirin). To reduce the pain, change your diet as stated in the food section. Be sure to exercise (increases blood flow and gets your immune system moving), stop smoking, interact with plants and animals, and avoid unnecessary antibiotic treatment (it kills the good as well as the bad microbes).

Brain health is vital. Salmon fish eggs or roe contains 3.5 more DHA than salmon meat. As a bonus the eggs contain zinc, iodine, and fat soluble K-2, D and A. To get more information go to www.lifeextensions.com. The government may take away DEHYDROEPIANDROSTERONE(DHEA). With your doctor's help, this hormone will save the brain and slow aging.

Don't forget SUNSHINE. Besides producing vitamin D, it stimulates all your systems.

PAIN

Seniors have a special need to control pain and stiffness. The key to control is to rewire your brain to accept pain. Use cognitive diffusion. You acknowledge your thoughts about pain without attacking them.

How do I do this? Meditate with guided imagery, use deep breathing (breathe in to the count of ten, hold for ten, exhale for ten and hold for ten) while eliciting a relaxation rather than a stress response to pain. Sit or lie down, close your eyes, concentrate on deep breathing while relaxing your muscles and live in the moment! DO NOT think of the past or the future, just NOW! Imagine a favorite resting place, i.e. the seashore, a garden, a place of nature. Some people want silence while others prefer soothing music. If you socialize, join a yoga or tai chi class. Again, it takes action, patience and vision. Stay away from drugs.

Consider LED light therapy, stem cell injections to grow new tissues. Injections of "sugar" solutions into damaged joints may help reduce pain. This process is called pro therapy. To find a doctor who will administer this protocol go to www. groprolo.com.

Research shows that wavelength light, 630-660 NM and 810-830 NM will help the enzyme CYTOCHOME C and OXYDASE triggering a healing process in the pain area. Read Dr. Richard Gerhauser's book "The Secrets of Underground Medicine". You can also review the websites www.joove.com or www.vielight.com for more details.

APPLE CIDER VINEGAR

Although ACV is acidic, it promotes an alkaline environment inside your body. ACV's use is versatile. As a food, it can be used as a marinade. When eating your leafy greens, use it as salad vinaigrette. Add a tang to your homemade cakes and candies. Wash fruit and vegetables in an ACV mix to remove pesticides, bacteria and viruses. Use to flavor vegetables, meats and soups. You can even make a hot beverage by mixing 2 tablespoons of ACV with 2 tablespoons lemon juice, 1 teaspoon cinnamon, 1 tablespoon honey and 12 ounces of hot live water.

If you have any problems, use it directly. Simply take a

tablespoon in water, hot or cold, before symptoms develop or eating. Be sure to rinse with plain water after so the acid does not affect your teeth.

It can be used to detoxify your liver (removes fat from and around the liver), lose weight (drink in the morning so it helps you feel full longer), use to pickle foods, and boost energy (the potassium and enzymes help relieve that tired feeling).

Be sure to buy the apple cider vinegar with the "mother" which is packed with enzymes, proteins, fiber and gut friendly probiotic bacteria with antioxidant, anti fungal and antibacterial properties.

It can also be used as a personal care product or cleaning agent.

There are numerous other books that list over a hundred different uses for ACV.

SLEEP

One third of American's report they are NOT getting enough sleep. Technically, we look at two (2) systems: glymphatic and circadian. The glymphatic system flushes out the toxins in the water soaked brain. When the brain is not cleaned, oxidants accumulate. Inflammation increases while amyloids and tau (proteins) are NOT removed. All of this increases the probability of Alzheimer's. (BAD)

The circadian sleep cycle regulates the hormones and microbiome. Sleep deprivation increases your appetite causing the brain to shrink and puts holes in your gut lining. The holes allow bacteria, etc., to enter the blood stream alarming the immune system to fight back. The war increases inflammation especially in the weakest part of your body. It's a vicious cycle.

The problems get worse. Lack of sleep increases the ghrelin hormone (it's the one that tells your body to eat more). The increased cortisol then spurs your appetite while at the same time lowering your leptin hormone which tells your brain that you are full (which helps you eat less). (Also BAD)

Deep sleep is very important for feeling rested and staying healthy. It supports short-term and long-term memory and overall learning. It's also when various hormones are secreted leading to growth and development of the body. It is during this stage that the brain cleans itself of toxins. You need to get roughly 1 to 2 hours of deep sleep per 8 hours of nightly sleep.

REM sleep is when we dream which is believed to be the way the brain processes and stores pieces of information relevant to previous events.

How do I improve sleep quality?

1. Have a dark quiet bedroom between 65 and 75 degrees F with 50 to 70% humidity. Have proper blankets, pillows and bedding that fit <u>your</u> body.
2. Establish a bedtime that allows 7-9 hours of sleep every day at during the same time.
3. Study and follow a dense nutrient rich natural diet.
4. Stop caffeine 8 hours <u>before</u> bedtime.
5. Try to avoid too much alcohol within 4 hours of sleep.

6. Avoid blue light after darkness and stop using screens at least 30 minutes before bed; 1-2 hours is better

7. Consider melatonin or other nutritional supplements.

8. Massage total body when you awaken (see other section).

9. You must get some sunlight in the morning shortly after awakening to stimulate the brain and trigger Vitamin D3 production that enhances the immune system.

10. Don't forget to exercise; it will tire you out and strengthen the core.

11. Do meditation procedure before bed. Go over the day's events emphasizing the positive. (What did I improve on or learn today?? Who did I help? What did I do to make my surroundings better?)

12. Train yourself like Pavlov's dog to have a set recital. Like hypnosis, it tells the brain it's time to sleep. I use the Lord's Prayer followed by loving moments with my wife as the sleep trigger.

13. If all else fails, consult with a doctor about sleep apnea testing.

Bottom line: sleep is vital. Your brain will be healthier and able to avoid memory loss, brain fog, obesity, and confusion. Remember 4-H. Believe head, heart, hands and health for making the best better and staying off the road to Hell of endless sleepless nights.

RELAXED MIND HEALTHY BODY

HERE'S ANOTHER APPROACH TO SUSTAIN LIFE

1. Time to Take Control. Now that you are retired, your health is your primary responsibility. It's Your Perception that matters. Be positive, have social engagements, help out in your Church, your community, or in a service capacity. Smile, Laugh!

2. The Varied Benefits of Meditation. Call it prayer, yoga, quiet time. Do it every day.

3. A Simple Program to Get Started With: find a quiet spot, use music and aromatherapy to engage your senses, just sit there and focus on one thought or a happy place and block out all others.

4. Being More Present: Remember the rule "You only have this moment. DO NOT GO BACK OR FORWARD".

5. Master the Flow State: Tapping into your innate, ultimate performance, your VISION OF "THE WAY". What is a flow state? It's when you gradually train your mind to flow like water to a peaceful serene place of inaction. The 'Default Mode Network' is when you will be like Pavlov's dog triggered to a sweet spot.

6. Besides meditation, DO NOT FORGET THE MORNING RITUAL of massaging yourself from head to toe.

7. Change Your Life Forever: with Cognitive Behavioral Therapy, you will sleep soundly, overcome anxiety, understand gratitude and how by giving, you will get more of what matters in life. Like meditation, it will assist entering a flow state of thought. Do not become discouraged. Remember a journey of a 1000 miles starts with a single step. Investigate the hundreds of books on the subject.

8. Don't forget music and smell to help you relax. Lavender is a favorite of many. As for music, classic is probably the most popular but experiment. A lot depends on what you were exposed to as a child.

AGING & ENERGY

All the health information is good, but I want to know how to slow the aging process. At the end of each strand of DNA is a telomere. Every time a cell divides, your telomere shortens. Your telomere runs cell division when it stops and you are toast (dead). Ever since the Chinese emperor had his alchemist work on an anti-aging potion (They failed but did discover gunpowder), man wants to find the distinction between mortal and immortal cell lines. Half of your telomeres burn off while you are still in the womb. As you age, shortened telomeres show "older" parts of your genome.

Dr. Blackburn, using single-cell organisms we know as pond scum, isolated an enzyme she called the telomerase. In short, telomerase rebuilds telomere that in time controls cell division.

FACT: If you artificially shorten the long telomere of young cells, you accelerate aging. Each cell is a little fire oxidizing glucose for energy. If the telomere become dysfunctional, the cells mitochondria that power the cell loses horsepower or becomes cancerous.

I assume you already have checked for iodine, selenium and zinc deficiencies and are eating right (see health section of K-1 and K-2 meds). Your doctor's blood test of homocysteine (amino acid that accumulates in your tissue) should show less than 15 micromoles per liter of blood. If high, start extra B12, folic acid, B6, B2 and TMG (trimethyl glycine). You can get B vitamins from proteins such as fish, poultry, meat, eggs, and dairy products. Leafy green vegetables, beans, and peas also have B vitamins.

Again, Chinese medicine shows that molecules in astragalus activated telomerase.

Besides astragalus, resveratrol (skin of red grapes) stimulates anti-aging genes called sirtuins. If you do not want the harmful effects of red wine, consume peanuts, raisins, mulberries, green tea (EGCG) and of course, N-acetyl cysteine (NAC).

If you are seriously failing, 1800 mg to 2400 mg of NAC will help as long as you had protected your gut's ability to absorb the foregoing substances. Carnosine (500 mgs) as well as L-arginine (that we discussed in the health section) stimulate the miracle molecule – nitric oxide. In conclusion, round out your supplements with an organic multivitamin containing C, D3, B12, gamma tocotrienol version of Vitamin E (there are 8 forms of Vitamin E so get the right one).

I am a meat-eater so I get Acetyl-L-carnitine from bacon and ground beef. If you are a vegetarian, consider 1000 mg of liquid l-carnitine. It is easier to absorb. The capsules using synthetic D- or DL-carnitine can interfere with the natural benefits.

Again balance and patience with exercise will slow the aging process. Remember the four levels (physical, mental, social and spiritual). Aging is influenced by all the forces. It requires balance. If you are social and pick up a virus, you could die. If you are a hermit, you lack stimulation and variety resulting in death. If you do not have spiritual purpose, standard habits you suffer stress from what you do not know and you die. If you do not have physical activities, your body weakens, your blood circulation slows, and bacteria are waiting to eat your flesh. So, it's all a trade off! The race of life is in your hands. The finish line is 6 feet underground. How you get there is up to you. (Remember the five principals in the youth section.) Only you have 100% control over your life. DO NOT LOSE CONTROL ON THE ONE TRIP DOWN THE RIVER OF LIFE. Tempus Fugit. (Time flies!)

Slowing the aging process is good but if one is always tired, life is still dull. What is the key to efficiently stroke the oxygen-to-carbon dioxide conversion (the fire of life)? We all know that infections, injuries, poor dietary habits, drugs, smoking, too much exercise, (which is a form of self-inflicted injury), or too little exercise causes the build up of toxins that damages our microchondria.

Research shows that all the above factors result in increased free radicals. When the cells (engine) is working efficiently like it does in children, the cells do not produce as many radicals. Unfortunately, as our cells replicate themselves, the life process becomes less efficient. Pharmaceutical companies push taking selenium, Vitamins A, C, E, antioxidants and lipoic acid. They do not slow aging because they do not attach directly the free radical accumulation. Enzymes do the job. Less oxygen results in less energy and the cells in turn produce less enzymes including superoxide, dismutase, catalyst, and glutathione, perofidase. It is a self-perpetuating cycle. Less energy, more free radicals and more free radicals result in less energy.

SOLUTION: Keep working. Proper exercise is the cheapest and easiest and most practical way to get more energy in your system. If absolutely necessary use oxygen therapy like OCONE or intravenous hydrogen treatment.

What is proper exercise? Simply walk fast for five minutes, pick up the pace for two minutes doing something like jumping jacks, push-ups, bending and swings. The goal is to get to the verge of being out of breath. This is scientifically known as the AEROBIC zone. Once this state is achieved run for one minute to increase the heartbeat and the lungs cleaned. End the protocol with three minutes of simple walking to recover. If tired, try centella, asiatica, ginkgo, bebols, acetyl l carnctino (ALCAR).

To help with diabetes take Solomon seed, berber flower, astragalius, licorice, milk thistle, white mulberry and wild yam roots.

To slow aging you want monolauren, elderberry, glycerol, lauricacid and NADT.

Secret: Harder and faster is not better.

WHERE ARE WE NOW???

What happened, fellow boomers? How did we fail? Did we walk too few hours? Did we fail to save? Did we invest poorly? It is not all your fault!!!

We worked hard averaging 42.4 hours per week while productivity nearly doubled between 1979 and 2013—less since then. The problem is that wages did not keep up with inflation. From 1948 through 1979, real wages adjusted for inflation but rose 93% since. After 1972, wages only increased 8% through 2009. After that, take home pay dropped because of rising taxes, cheap foreign imports; low food and commodity values declined.

During the same period, people took on MORE debt and saved less. By the early 2000s, we saved less than 1% of our income. Because disposable take home pay did not increase to satisfy the "keep up with the Jones'" mentality, we took on credit card, home equity, balloon loans to increase interest rate after 5 years and student loans etc. until debt service ratio went from less than 10% to 13% in 2009. Then the bubble burst and people defaulted, refinanced or went bankrupt. These problems caused an increase in inequality and envy between the races.

The present problem is compounded by the fact that people invested poorly. While the S&P stock index has averaged 11% since the mid 1980s, the average investor earned only 3.7%. WHY: poorly informed people chose returns. Buy high, sell low (bad). Like me, they cling onto a sinking stock hoping for a turnaround. They got crushed by the "dot com" bubble when the NASDAQ lost 78% between 2000 to 2002. People are trapped in lousy 401 plans, company stock, etc. Even though our investments were poor with high fee annuities, to satisfy our spouses and children, we attempted to live well beyond our means. We over leveraged to buy bigger houses, faster cars and a more luxurious life style. All of this put us on the path into Hell.

Where are we now? Many companies to save money have taken away defined benefit plans and many have replace it with a 401k. Is your company paying ito a certain plan?? Check it out! Many people have no retirement program. Millions live on Social Security alone (about $20,000 per year for the "average couple over 65 assuming they did NOT take it at 62). The "average" retiree has a net worth of around $300,000 with about ½ in retirement accounts earning $5000 per year (If you take out principal to live on, you earn less). If you are in fixed income assets (CDs, bonds), the government has declared low interest rates until at least 2023. Government policy has forced retirees into stock and real estate.

One third of retirees get a third source of income: a pension. Private ones pay about $10,000 per year with government pensions paying out about $25,000 (notice the difference; one reason for tension). Illinois is an example of why: it cannot pay its pensions unless it raises more taxes.

Here is the source of fear. If you do not own your home free and clear of debt, you have $5000 in investment income, $25,000 from Social Security and no pension (unless you are in the 1/3 that does have a pension). Assume one of a couple has a $20,000 per year pension. Now you have $5,000 plus $25,000, and $20,000 for a total of $50,000 per year.

If you do not own your home with no debt, your yearly expenses could be $15,000 for rent or mortgage payments, $3000 for utilities, $15,000 for food (at home or eating out), clothes, $2000 for car expenses (insurance, gas), plus $5000 depreciation of one vehicle, and $15,000 for health care and insurance assuming no major operations or keeping a reserve for a nursing home.

Now you have $50,000 with $55,000 in basic expenses. Already you are in a deficit with no quality items like travel, golf, supporting grandchildren, etc. Now you know why so many know they cannot retire but must continue to work. Face the fact and the odiousness of working will dissipate. Plan now for future living arrangements. Check out the cost of living in Tennessee versus Anaheim, California or San Francisco versus Thomson, Illinois. Be realistic about your stock returns. DO NOT crash, panic or use short term strategies hoping to catch a big payoff (Tesla, Microsoft, Square, etc.). Stay healthy to avoid medical expenses. Take advantage of coupons, Groupons, AARP discounts, etc. Start spending your savings. You cannot take it with you when you die. Decide what you really need to be happy and sell the rest. Do not give the Devil what he wants.

INVESTING IN AN AGE
OF UNCERTAINTY

The approach and risk level is very different when you are 20 than when you are 60. The world has changed. The old standard of 60% in bonds or income producing instruments (CDs) and 40% in "blue" chip stock is outdated. The Federal Reserve through quantitative easing has crunched yields and inflated the stock market by pumping trillions of fake money into companies.

The purpose is noble. It is designed to stabilize the real economy by saving jobs. People with jobs have money to spend. This in turn creates demand for goods and services. The Federal Reserve wants demand. It wants the velocity. Velocity is a measure of how many times the same dollar can be used to purchase the same number of goods. When there is more money than goods, the demand for existing goods increases creating inflation. The Fed wants 2% inflation per year. More than that in their minds creates unstable speculation and hoarding of real assets. The Fed, in order to avoid current deflation (assets costing fewer dollars) has actively purchased Treasury bonds and NOW junk corporate debt. Their purchases have created a grossly expanded clearing house for their assets ABOVE their true market value. This allows the bank to profit buyer and selling shifting the loss to the taxpayers. Big problem. The banks make the rich richer when there is a profit and dump the losses to the taxpayers when they have losers. The normal market cycles of having deflation to balance inflation has been suspended. The U.S. dollar, being the world's reserve currency, has aided and abetted the stability and peace the elite want.

The picture has further been clouded by the Bureau of Labor "moving the goalposts" when reporting the consumer price index. By substituting items in the consumer bracket (steak for chicken) and having the federal treasury borrowing paper currency to subsidize low good prices, housing etc., the index appears to stabilize the economy. The bottom line's real value is destroyed as persistent inflation gives debt loss a windfall reduction in the value of the DEBT they owe. Bankers, like alchemists, keep trying to turn lead into gold. The inflation tax simply consumes capital.

Since 1913, the banks have succeeded because productivity via technology has increased supply. Globalization has opened up new markets and cheaper raw materials. Health advances have allowed millions of children to grow up as consumers.

All of this has disguised the risk and rewarded expanded leverage (more debt). In the race to the end, any investor can lend and borrow an unlimited amount at a risk free rate of interest. The party will continue until something (Black Swan) burst the bubble and ends the party. The effect will be like when ice melts at 32 degrees and the solid river you walked over on turns to a rushing stream of water eroding the soil and carrying away the house you built too close to the river bank.

Enough theory. What does this mean for a senior investor?

1. You must diversify. If you have over a million dollars put 30% outside the reach of the U.S. government dollar.
2. In a crisis, the government will protect the status quo and kick the can down the road with MORE debt.
3. Government attention in the short term is to keep power and get reelected. YOU must look <u>long</u> term in real company producing <u>real</u> goods and services.
4. Gold and land are optimal stores of value. Put 10%-50% into those assets depending on how much capital you have (do NOT over leverage at the senior level 60+)
5. Crashes and bubbles happen more frequently now. The market is a pendulum swinging from fear to greed and back. Wall Street is a rigged game. Brokers are salesmen with an inventory to sell to suckers. Stay skeptical. NO ONE will guard your assets like you do.
6. There is NO free lunch. Someone must pay NOW or in the future. Take advantage of the government policies even when they are not in the country's best interest.
7. Stay with stocks that make money NOW, that pay a dividend, have real cash flow and a debt level below 50% of company net worth.
8. On real estate, if you do not want to manage your own properties, go with REIT (Real Estate Investment Trust) that have low debt, dividends below earnings level and not commercial malls or office buildings. Amazon and Zoom have changed the demand level forever.

It will NOT be easy. Study and get different opinions and adjust the sale of assets to meet your age, spending requirements, and interest.

A PENNY SAVED IS A PENNY EARNED WITHOUT TAXES

Keeping your needs small is the key to keeping off the path to Hell on earth. Everywhere you turn someone is trying to sell you something. First, never buy on impulse. Stores and marketing experts study everyone to trick you into buying. Where do they put the milk in a store? Way in the back. Where do they place generic food items: on the bottom shelf. Where do they put candy and cold soda: right where you must stand in line to check out. Avoid the temptation. Shop for groceries on a full stomach. Have a list of what you need. Stay away from the processed foods. Buy in bulk at Costco or Sam's (only buy what you will really use before expiration dates).

How do I keep my needs small? After you have written down what you _really_ need to be happy, you need to follow these rules.

1. Try not to buy new. Use the thrift, Goodwill, Salvation Army and the internet (eBay, Craig's List), etc. to find what you need. Today the world is your market place.
2. Always request senior discounts. ASK, ASK and ASK AGAIN for bargains. Measure time versus savings.
3. Use a Citi Card currently a double cash credit card giving a 2% discount on everything or Discover giving

5% back on items changing each quarter (this quarter is restaurants; next quarter gas). Check the internet for incentives (Southwest had a great point bonus if you were able to fly). ALWAYS PAY OFF your credit cards every month. The banks want you to use credit to charge high interest and late fees; do NOT get trapped.

4. Look to government subsidies. Today the government is wild with subsidies, housing, food, utilities, farm subsidies, solar installation, etc. ASK local, country, state and national agencies. There are hundreds of articles on the internet to explore for money. Veterans, students and seniors have tons of serious giveaways, if you take the time to find them.

5. Look to private entities. Churches are an easy target for bleeding hearts. Lions Club and other service clubs have programs for the blind, sick and disabled. Youth: Don't forget unions and AARP. Take extra care to see if your past employer, fraternity club (Moose, Eagles, Elks) have any benefits.

6. Keep your eyes open and your ears alert for people dying or going to a nursing home. Funeral homes, lawyers, churches, senior organizations are excellent sources for intelligence on who has fallen and where to "help" their families dispose of excess material (especially furniture, clothes, cars, adult toys like golf clubs, time shares, etc.)

As a senior, you probably do not need scholarships but your grandchildren might. (Remember many schools provide free classes for Seniors to audit). The scholarships are in the millions. Check out the internet and library for information. There are scholarships for dwarfs, bowlers, golfers, nurses, jewelry makers, Lutheran women, scuba divers, etc. The list goes on and on. Use the library: it's free and can get you all sorts of services through inter-library loans. Never buy new books again: use the library's or barter with others or support your used book store.

Enough generalities; you want specifics.

A. Get free or low-cost drugs from Partnerships for Prescriptions: www.pparx.org; Needy Meds: www.NeedyMeds.org; RxAssist: www.rxassist.org; Center for Benefits Access: https://www.ncoa.org/centerforbenefits/; RxHope: www.rxhope.com; RxOutreach: https://rxoutreach.org/; GoodRx: www.goodrx.com or others. Check out what discounts your pharmacy offers.

B. You need exercise but be sure to stay within your capabilities; stop before you get sore and gradually increase your challenge. You will enjoy it more and then tend to stick with the program. Use Yoga Today or another free online fitness class; that's cheaper than a gym fitness center unless your Medicare plan offers Silver Sneakers.

C. Find a dental school nearby and have a "supervised student" take care of your teeth. (Iowa City charges 70% of the state average costs.) Medicaid (green card) offers help for free.

D. Visit Eyecare America: https://www.aao.org/eyecare-america or your local Lion's Club for eye care.

E. Want to travel? Go to Trusted House Sitters (https://www.trustedhousesitters.com/) to watch someone's house, plants, pets, etc.

F. If you are scared or afraid to fight over crooked bills, then here is a "bill haggler" (cheaper than a lawyer unless you go to legal aid). There are companies like Billshark and BillFixers who for a fee will negotiate a problem for you.

G. Don't forget to get your senior homestead real estate tax break; many states offer reductions for veterans, seniors or the disabled. Also check on lower car license plate and car registration fees.

H. Streaming (Roku, Hulu, Netflix, Amazon Prime) and cable TV are charging you every month. Again ASK and switch (are you really using all 58 channels?!)

I. Download books to read: check out Project Gutenberg: http://gutenberg.org/ They have over 60,000 free eBooks. Your library offers eBooks and audio books. Amazon Prime offers free Kindle books; be careful that you don't "borrow" a book that requires a membership.

J. Maximize coupons. Use Ibotta, Shopmium or Honey to save real money.

K. Check out Card Cash (www.cardcash.com/) or Cardpool (www.cardpool.com) to buy gift cards at a discount.

L. Stop smoking or if not, then roll your own. Buy tobacco by the pound. You can also buy "tubes" but you will need a tobacco injector filling machine.

M. Use Amazon Prime Day for bargains.

N. Check local websites for cheap or free events where you live (do not forget the university and college offerings).

O. Compare your cell phone with a prepaid phone; depending on your usage needs, the prepaid phone might save you money.

P. Go to Shoptagr website to link to online stores.

Q. Plant a garden and reduce your lawn. Use patio or rock instead of grass.

R. Veterans, go to Military Benefits for information on discounts.

S. Get a roommate and split expenses.

Remember: IT IS YOUR MONEY SO SAVE WISELY.

When eating out, consider the following. It will encourage you to eat wholesome food.

Often the same restaurant will have two different sets of prices for the same meal at different times of the day. Go during the happy hour period between 3 p.m. and 7 p.m., you can often order the same kinds of entrees, but without paying the big entrée prices.

Coupons are another great way to save, and one that many people never take advantage of. Websites like Couponsherpa, Groupon and others have plenty of deals listed on their Web pages each day. Don't forget restaurant.com.

When renting a car, book the cheapest one. Everyone wants those, so the company will be most likely to be out of stock and upgrade you. For the best shot, go early in the day before most people have returned their cars. The agent may try to sell you a nicer car for an upcharge, but if you refuse, he has no choice but to give you a better model for free.

Open two IRAs right now. Show this to your children and grandchildren to start early. Got your 401(k) sorted? Great. Now open a traditional IRA and a Roth IRA immediately. You can always put money into an IRA, even if you have a workplace plan. If you have previous 401(k) plans, you can roll them over into the IRA to grow the balance and manage them yourself. A Roth IRA is not tax deductible and subject to an income test, the growth is tax-free and withdrawals later are also tax-free, forever..

HSA or flex: Health Saving Plans are a must unless your employers have a good group plan. The health care business is changing fast, and the tax laws are moving to keep up. Your workplace probably offers a flexible spending account (FSA), a health savings account (HAS) or both. An HSA is coupled with a high-deductible health insurance plan. Families can set aside up to $6,900 a year, and the money rolls over each year. It can even be invested and is never taxed so long as you spend it on health care needs.

Avoid short term, go long term. This seems like it might go without saying, but avoid selling a stock sooner than 12 months. If you hold a stock for at least one year, it will be taxed at 0%, 15% or 20%, depending on your total taxable income. If you sell before one year has passed, even by one day, you are taxed at your prevailing income tax rate on the gain, from 10% up to 37%.

Your Income Tax Rate	Long-Term Capital Gains Rate	Short-Term Capital Gains Rate
10%	0%	10%
15%	0%	15%
25%	15%	25%
28%	15%	28%
33%	15%	33%
35%	15%	35%
39.60%	20%	39.60%

The rate you pay on an investment gain is determined by your taxable income in the year you sell, and whether you held the stock for more or less than one year. Less than one year and you pay the short-term rate, equal to your income tax rate. Holding longer qualifies you for the lower long-term rate.

SOURCE: IRS

Make the most of your affiliations: AARP, military, union, etc. Be a regular and ASK, ASK and ASK again for VIP treatment.

Finally in another section, I discuss benefits of running a business. You can do it even after retirement. Remember a penny saved is much better than a penny earned because to ear the penny, you give 10% to 50% of it to the state and federal income taxes.

Okay, we have the general philosophy. Now where are the specifics? If you have more than $1,000,000 in net worth, you know how the game is played or have enough to get good advice. Make sure you study three different plans and advise. Verify past performance. Diversify between three approaches to wealth and security. You do not have the time to recover.

When You Take Benefits: It All Adds Up

	Begin Age 62 (Monthly Benefits $750)	Begin Age 66 (Monthly Benefits $1,000)	Begin Age 70 (Monthly Benefits $1,320)
Live to 70	$72,000	$48,000	$0
Live to 75	$117,000	$108,000	$79,200
Live to 78	$144,000	$144,000	$126,720
Live to 83	$189,000	$204,000	$205,920
Live to 85	$207,000	$228,000	$237,600
Live to 90	$252,000	$288,000	$316,800
Live to 95	$297,000	$348,000	$396,100

Still, as the table above demonstrates, putting off filing for benefits has long-term implications that become more and more dramatic, the longer you live. The difference for someone living until the age of 90, if one files at age 62 versus age 70, is more than $60,000. For someone who lives until age 95, it equals nearly $100,000 in additional benefit payments.

I.   Look at the chart on Social Security benefits. If you are working, stop at least around 66-67 to get full benefits. If you must work to live or have passion enjoying your work, DO NOT TAKE SOCIAL SECURITY UNTIL 70. Talk to the government about survival and spousal benefits; very important. Maybe you divorced??? Definitely take it at 70; it's a no brainer. I was retired at 52 so I took mine at 62 because I wanted to enjoy the money. Do not expect to live past 78 and know the purchasing power of the money in 2002 was greater than the value in 2020. I saw too many clients who saved and delayed only to get sick or disabled and unable to enjoy the money.

II.   Take Medicare at 65 and investigate a supplement plan. If you are very healthy, you can forego the supplement or enroll in a high deductible to cover the "big" expense of cancer, stroke, etc. If you are taking drugs at 65, enroll in part "D" to cover prescriptions. In my opinion, I want natural cures and avoid prescriptions and did NOT enroll. My wife who at 62 developed diabetes enrolled in "D".

III.   If you have family support, or are wealthy enough do NOT waste money on a nursing home, i.e. a long term care plan or burial insurance. STAY in your home; that's my preference and I will donate my body to science and let them pay the cremation costs.

IV.   This Form 4 was created under Section 16(a) of the Securities Exchange Act to keep insiders "honest". It states that when a C-level executive—such as a CEO, COO or CFO—or any board member of a company wants to buy shares of his or her company's stock, they can do so legally. They just have to fill out the Firm 4 within two days of making the trade. These investors are always ahead of the game. They get in BEFORE every big announcement...BEFORE billionaires like Oprah and Buffett sweep in and bid up the stock. Go to the U.S. Securities and Exchange Commission website (www.sec.gov) to study insiders buys of stock with the insiders' own money.

How to Access the Form 4

1. Type www.sec.gov into your internet browser. It takes you to the U.S. SEC's website.
2. There is a link about halfway down the page that says "EDGAR/Company filings." In the entry box next to it, type in the name or stock symbol of the company you're searching for and hit return.
3. On the upper left of the webpage, look for the words "insider transactions" (hint: it's highlighted in red) and click on it.
4. The next page that comes up lists all the insider transactions for the company.
5. You can click on the filing number for each owner to access the Form 4s they've filed.

Form 144: Companies sometimes hand out restricted stock, or otherwise "unregistered" securities. If you were an insider and wanted to sell more than 500 shares (or securities with a value of $10,000 or more), you would fill out a Form 144.

Keep in mind, the insider isn't obligated to sell those shares. But once a Form 144 is filed with the SEC, the insider has three months to follow through on the sale of the securities.

V. I studied many historical charts all the way back to 1870. I analyzed the panic of 1907, the collapse of 1929-1932, and the set back of 1937. Then I studied the cycles of the baby boomers. Between 1992 and 2011, the average investor made 8.6% per year on oil stocks; 8.8% per year on the S &P 500 stocks; 7.7% on gold bullion, only 2.3% on his home depending upon location; and suffered a 2.6% per year loss due to inflation. Why did the average investor do so poorly?? He lacked true diversity, held on to losers hoping for a comeback, buying after the elite used insider information, was sucked into a pump and dump stock paying too high fees and over trading. He was competing against the brightest minds in the world armed with sophisticated computers, dark trades, government corruption, foreign interference and a floating dollar! DO NOT believe all the advisors promising to make 50-100% annual returns. If they could really do that, would they be selling us fear in a $3000 per year internet service? Get real. In short, do not move more than 40% of your insolvent dollar in individual stocks. Stick with Vanguard.

If you want to play, make sure the stocks pay a dividend, has a reasonable debt, a profit to earning ratio below 15 to 1. It needs to be a leader in its sector. Examples in October 2020: Microsoft MST, Walmart WMT, Costco COST, McDonald's MCD, Clorox CHX, Disney DIS, Apple AAP:, United Technologies UTX, Johnson & Johnson JNJ. To add returns, sell cover calls 60-90 days out for more income. If called away, buy within 30 to avoid capital gains and sell a high strike price. DO NOT FIGHT the Federal Reserve. When they reverse policy and tighten credit, go to cash and buy short term treasury funds. I use SCHO but Fidelity and Goldman Sachs have similar products. Use E trade, Fidelity or Interactive brokers to save on commissions.

VI.   Spend money that is outside your IRA and 401K plan so that the money in them continues to grow tax deferred.

VII. Show these charts to your grandchildren. Help them understand (and give them money if necessary) that they need to put money into their IRAs and 401K plans as early as possible. Lawrence opens a tax-deferred retirement account at age 26. He invests $3,000 per year in this account for 40 consecutive years. Lawrence stops contributing at age 65. His account grows at 9% per year.

Sally opens a tax deferred retirement account at age 18. She invests $3,000 per year in this account for eight consecutive years. After those eight years, she makes no more contributions to her retirement account and her account grows at 9% per year. The results of these two approaches are below…and

Age	Robert		Sally	
	Contribution	Year-End Value	Contribution	Year-End Value
16	$0	$0	$0	$0
17	$0	$0	$0	$0
18	$0	$0	$3,000	$3,270
19	$0	$0	$3,000	$6,834
20	$0	$0	$3,000	$10,719
21	$0	$0	$3,000	$14,954
22	$0	$0	$3,000	$19,570
23	$0	$0	$3,000	$24,601
24	$0	$0	$3,000	$30,085
25	$0	$0	$3,000	$36,063
26	$3,000	$3,270	$0	$39,309
27	$3,000	$6,834	$0	$42,847
28	$3,000	$10,719	$0	$46,703
29	$3,000	$14,954	$0	$50,906
30	$3,000	$19,570	$0	$55,488
31	$3,000	$24,601	$0	$60,481
32	$3,000	$30,085	$0	$65,925
33	$3,000	$36,063	$0	$71,858
34	$3,000	$42,579	$0	$78,325
35	$3,000	$49,681	$0	$85,374
36	$3,000	$57,422	$0	$93,058
37	$3,000	$65,860	$0	$101,433
38	$3,000	$75,058	$0	$110,562
39	$3,000	$85,083	$0	$120,513

40	$3,000	$96,010	$0	$131,359
41	$3,000	$107,921	$0	$143,182
42	$3,000	$120,904	$0	$156,068
43	$3,000	$135,055	$0	$170,114
44	$3,000	$150,480	$0	$185,424
45	$3,000	$167,294	$0	$202,112
46	$3,000	$185,620	$0	$220,303
47	$3,000	$205,596	$0	$240,130
48	$3,000	$227,369	$0	$261,742
49	$3,000	$251,103	$0	$285,298
50	$3,000	$276,972	$0	$310,975
51	$3,000	$305,169	$0	$338,963
52	$3,000	$335,905	$0	$369,470
53	$3,000	$369,406	$0	$402,722
54	$3,000	$405,923	$0	$438,967
55	$3,000	$445,726	$0	$478,474
56	$3,000	$489,111	$0	$521,536
57	$3,000	$536,401	$0	$568,475
58	$3,000	$587,947	$0	$619,637
59	$3,000	$644,132	$0	$675,405
60	$3,000	$705,374	$0	$736,191
61	$3,000	$772,128	$0	$802,448
62	$3,000	$844,889	$0	$874,669
63	$3,000	$924,199	$0	$953,389
64	$3,000	$1,010,647	$0	$1,039,194
65	$3,000	$1,104,876	$0	$1,132,721
Less Total Invested		**-$120,000**		**-$24,000**
Net Earnings		**$984,876**		**$1,108,721**
Return on Money		**8-fold**		**46-fold**

THEY ARE EXTRAORDINARY!

Sally made just eight contributions of $3,000, for a total of $24,000 invested. Lawrence made 40 contributions of $3,000 for a total of $120,000 invested. NOW THEY KNOW HOW COMPOUND INTEREST REALLY WORKS!!!

I hired my daughter at 16 to work in the office and made her fund a Roth IRA. Now you put in $6,000 rather than the $3,000 per year. Better yet, get your children and grandchildren who work (must be earned income) and have them fund both a regular IRA and a Roth IRA. If the government does not nationalize private pensions, my daughter will have a $1,000,000 pension at 65. Sadly inflation and taxes may destroy it all so do what the rich do in VIII.

VIII. Buy farmland, duplexes, 4-plexes, forest, or land in the pathway of development. Regardless of what the dollar does, REAL ASSETS HAVE REAL VALUE.

IX. Buy delinquent real estate taxes. Go to the country court house and learn the rules. Call me at 815-259-3168 for free advise on how to earn 4% to 36% per year on liens superior to the bank's mortgage.

X.   Buy gold jewelry at bullion prices. This is a specialty where you must be VERY CAREFUL. Today gold plated or covered can fake you out. Even silver dollars can be fake. Ten years ago, I bought US silver dollars in Prague, CZ valued at $7 a piece. I demanded the "dealer" tell me how could he do it (were they stolen?) He shocked me when he told me they were silver plated struck in Russia. "Clever dudes". By buying jewelry at bullion prices, you have: A. Real value, B. Jewelry like art goes up in value; C. You can wear and enjoy it or use it to escape out of the city when riots begin.

XI. Finally, you need a survival plan in investing. We already covered the need for a least a three (3) month survival cash plan (fund children). If you can afford it and a survival kit with essentials to go to a predetermined safe house. (There are all kinds of books, guides and manuals). Don't go crazy but know your capabilities. Don't expect to be a hunter, fisherman, "John Wayne" if you have not prepared and practiced. Buying a gun is NOT being a marksman. When I was in the JAG (USAR), I thought firing a 45 caliber would be like it is on TV. No Way! It is tough to hit the target at 50'. I was like the bad guys in the movies who never hit the star of the show.

In summary, DO THE FOLLOWING by investing in your family. It is the best form of investing and the returns cannot be measured in dollars.

1. Have a safe place outside the bank to store a reasonable amount of currency, gold, and silver. I have a bag of junk 10 cent, 25 cent and 50 cent coins to spend (people will recognize them). I also have cigarettes and whiskey to barter with.

2. Become less "U.S.-dependent" by holding assets overseas and/or having a plan to evacuate to another country. Visit first. Greece, Portugal, Croatia, southern France are good locations. Uruguay is my favorite because there is FOOD there. Remember, in a crisis there may be NO planes to transport you.

3. Keep a 30-day supply of cash, medicines, food, water and guns and ammunition. I like organic honey as it does NOT spoil and will also serve to heal wounds. Put oats in the honey jar to have protein that will last 100 years.

4. Find a way to get to any of the 50 or so places in the country that have real concentrations of wealth or buy farmland or arrange NOW a relocate where you can get to with ½ a tank of gas to protect your family.

5. Review your critical documents (birth certificate, passport, will, health power, property power, life insurance, beneficiary on your pension and annuities, bank account and the key to your lock boxes) once a year.

6. Do not hold bonds.

7. Be very cautious buying life, funeral, or long term care insurance.

8. If you have talents, skill and want part-time work, look at the opportunities on Elance.com, odeck.com, Freelancer.com.

9. Own your own "asset-light" business. See section earlier in the book.

10. Focus your stock investing on "Trophy Assets" and capital-efficient businesses. Know the intrinsic value of your dividends and cover calls.

11. I reminded you earlier that without health, you don't need this section; you are dead or have Alzheimer's. Four new items that I have added to my life are music (Mozart and Baroque), blueberries and avocados and other nutrient dense foods and massages. My legs have pain and I need to reduce inflammation and modulate the immune system. The fourth is N-acetylcysteine. It is a booster to increase glutathione stores in the liver. It binds carcinogenic substances (cancer) in these toxins and eliminates them through urine and bile.

HOW TO DRAW A NEW PATH
AWAY FROM HELL

The second most translated book after the Bible is TAO TE CHING, a collection of 81 poems describing the way of the universe and life. In contrast to this book of action, it is about the wisdom of inaction. It ponders the acceptance of what you cannot change, i.e. death of a loved one, the state of the economy, or the behavior of others. The symbol of Tao is two phases of the moon conjoined. It emphasizes the balance of light and dark, action and inaction, feminine and masculine. The Way does not educate but shows you when you know you don't know, you will find your own path in avoiding Hell on earth. Our nature should be like water: forceful, yet always first to yield by moving around barriers and relentlessly seeking the simplest path. The landscape can be transformed by eroding the mountain before you.

If you are happy, you have mastered yourself. If you know yourself, you have true wisdom. When you are on the path to serenity, you do not need others' approval. You don't need to chase money or security. When your life is full of responsibilities and obligations while technology and the rat race of modern life puts unnecessary anxiety and pressure on your soul, you need serenity NOW. You are retired, the race is over, you are free if you can work with change and not fight against it.

To find the way, you need resilience. How do you achieve the "Way".

1. Have tight feedback loops.
2. Cluster your needed resources close by while maintaining diversity. It is a trade off of how efficient do you need to be without sacrificing diversity.
3. 90% of us are thin 10 miles of a Walmart. What happens when Walmart kills off the other supply chains in the area???
4. Reorganization when a black swan hits (virus). How can the system adapt to meet the needs?
5. Relocation: if something happens, how easy is it to move to a safer place?

Enough theory. How do I achieve the "Way"?

A. Think about the last time you were truly happy.
B. What did you think life in the future would be like when you were 10? When you were 30? What do my interests, hobbies and role models have in common?

If you have fears or pain, you need to define/specify what they are. Reflect NOW on what you fear now. Stay focused. Temptation and evil will try to pull you off the pathway. What is holding you back? Maybe retirement requires a lifestyle change. Maybe it means removing all the things making your goals difficult to achieve. Maybe you need to physically move to a new location or go back to your birthplace to grow new roots. Maybe you need to change jobs, divorce your mate, change relationships with your children. Help yourself establish disciplined habits. It can be as simple as making your bed every single morning, exercising everyday at the same time and place. Maybe it's ride sharing to reduce the cost and stress of commuting to work. Maybe it is learning a new skill, joining a new church or service club.

YOU DECIDE. BE LIKE WATER, FLOWING DOWN THE RIVER OF LIFE. ACTION WILL LEAD YOU TO INACTION.

Remember the third rule of life from Part I. The Only thing you have 100% control is YOURSELF. You have to take action. Do Not give out. The worst thing to do is give up. You will regret what might have been. Balance action with inaction. The following poem gives you a point of reflection.

Invictus

..It matter not how strait the gate,
How charged the punishments the scroll.
I am the master of my fate:
I am the captain of my soul. -William Ernest Henley

OMEGA

The end as in death is certain.

It is easy to live in remembrance of the past or in preparation of tomorrow; thereby losing TODAY. Many people deny death; living as though they will live forever, making it easy to postpone the things you know you must do. You must give up everything in order to gain everything. You can only be yourself if you are no one else. You do not need my approval to be you. I had two aunts who were "saints", but never married because no one met their mother's approval. When they died at 89, they still had their "hope chest" that I keep as a reminder of missed opportunities. A full life of love and giving and children were lost. Society lost. We lost because their full potential was never achieved. Do NOT become a captive of cultural defined role expectations. So many people settle down and forfeit their dreams and visions for a better world. Continue to grow. Let the Force guide you to the power and strength within you and then use it to do the right thing in each situation. That is Wisdom.

At the beginning of this treatise, I stated I wished a mentor had given me a recipe for living. In researching the recesses of my mind, I remember the oral advice my father gave me when on June 10, 1968, the day I left for college on the train for Trinity College, Connecticut. A place I had never seen and where I knew no one. My dad's advice was simple but it is the rock that I built my life on: NEVER GIVE UP.

WORDS OF WISDOM

"The Hunger for love is much more difficult to remove than the hunger for bread." --Mother Teresa

"I think we consider too much the good luck of the early bird and not enough the bad luck of the early worm." -Franklin D. Roosevelt

"When you rush to get to a mythical 'there', one day you will arrive and realize you missed all of the pleasures and mysteries along the way." --James Altucher

"Know your own happiness. Want for nothing but patience – or give it a more fascinating name: Call it hope."
--Jane Austen

"Your beliefs become your thoughts,
Your thoughts become your words,
Your words become your actions,
Your actions become your habits,
Your habits become your values,
Your values become your destiny." --Mahatma Gandhi

CONCLUSION FOR PART III

Wait two days and study the introduction and conclusion in PART I. The lessons are the same whether you are 18 or 81. The sands of time slip away. A life well lived will have a basket of warm memories and a brightness of dreams for tomorrow. The light will help you off the path of darkness, selfishness and Hell. DO NOT GIVE UP. You have one ride down the river of Life. Think of Life as a race with the finish line six feet underground. Enjoy the race or your river ride. Time and Tide wait for no man.

Lawrence Bruckner Esq.
Bruck175@hotmail.com